CONSULTATION

Creating School-Based Interventions

Third Edition

Don Dinkmeyer, Jr. and Jon Carlson

Routledge
Taylor & Francis Group
New York   London

BP53

Published in 2006 by
Routledge
Taylor & Francis Group
270 Madison Avenue
New York, NY 10016

Published in Great Britain by
Routledge
Taylor & Francis Group
2 Park Square
Milton Park, Abingdon
Oxon OX14 4RN

© 2006 by Taylor & Francis Group, LLC
Routledge is an imprint of Taylor & Francis Group

Printed in the United States of America on acid-free paper
10 9 8 7 6 5 4 3 2 1

International Standard Book Number-10: 0-415-95198-4 (Softcover)
International Standard Book Number-13: 978-0-415-95198-2 (Softcover)
Library of Congress Card Number 2005014225

Library of Congress Cataloging-in-Publication Data

Dinkmeyer, Don C., 1952-
    Consultation : creating school-based interventions / Don Dinkmeyer, Jon Carlson.--3rd ed.
        p. cm.
    Includes index.
    ISBN 0-415-95198-4 (pb : alk. paper)
    1. School children--Mental health services. 2. Mental health consultation. 3. Student counselors.
4. Adlerian psychology. 5. Educational counseling. I. Carlson, Jon. II. Title.

LB3430.D55 2005
371.7'13--dc22

2005014225

Taylor & Francis Group
is the Academic Division of T&F Informa plc.

Visit the Taylor & Francis Web site at
http://www.taylorandfrancis.com

and the Routledge Web site at
http://www.routledge-ny.com

7/12/06

To Don Dinkmeyer, Sr.
For his dedication to Individual Psychology.
For his leadership, encouragement, and modeling
of consultation skills.

CONTENTS

FOREWORD

It was a great pleasure to have been asked to write the foreword to this book on consultation, as consulting has occupied more than half of my career, beginning in 1956 when I consulted with the Ventura School for Girls, a California Youth Authority School for older adolescent girls, and then continuing for the next 11 years. My last major consultation was with the Schwab Middle School in Cincinnati, Ohio, where I spent about 95 days of the 1994–1995 school year working in the school.

As I read through this book, my whole career as a consultant flashed through my mind. Although I am not an Adlerian, the reality therapy I practice is reasonably close. I can easily relate to everything Dinkmeyer and Carlson have explained in this book. Here, in a short book, are explanations of all the things I have learned the hard way over almost 50 years of consulting.

If you are asked into a school to help teachers and counselors deal with students who are not doing as they are told, and this will comprise 99 percent of the people you will be asked to help schools deal with, here is a book that will take you through the process for almost any kind of situation you will encounter.

As an experienced consultant, I would like to consult with you, the potential reader of this book: Pay attention to what is written here. You will still have to learn a lot the hard way, but not nearly as much as I struggled to learn over the years because I did not have access to what is so clearly explained in this book.

William Glasser
President of the William Glasser Institute in Chatsworth, California

PREFACE

Consultation: Creating School-Based Interventions is for school personnel who work with teachers, students, parents, and administrators in
our school systems. We believe that school counselors and psychologists are most likely to be in this role. All four populations expect service and consultation is an effective means to meeting their needs. A
consultation relationship has become the relationship of choice.

Consultation has been a "mandated" function of school counselors
and school psychologists for many years. The American School Counselor Association (ASCA) and the National Association of School
Psychologists (NASP) have included consultation as a major function
in their policy statements. The recent movement by the ASCA to rede-
fine the school counselor's role absolutely emphasizes consultation
skills. Yet decades later, consultants still seek effective ideas for this
essential role.

This book gives mental health professionals a set of consultation
skills for working with these populations. We have focused a skill into
each chapter, and expect the reader to be unfamiliar with many of our
ideas. These ideas come from Adlerian or Individual Psychology, and
we are grateful to those who preceded our works in this field of psychology. Individual Psychology has a rich tradition of working in the
schools and with parents. This book represents a new synthesis of the
ideas for all of the school populations.

Both authors are profoundly grateful to Don Dinkmeyer, Sr. He
served as the first author in the first version of this book (Dinkmeyer, D.
& Carlson, J. (1973). *Consulting: Facilitating human potential and
change.* Columbus, OH: Charles Merrill), coauthored the second

(Dinkmeyer, D., Carlson, J., & Dinkmeyer, D., Sr. (1994). *Consultation: School mental health professionals as consultants.* Muncie, IN: Accelerated Development) and was an inspiration as we created this version.

We bring more than 85 years of experience, including work in literally all 50 states, Canada, and internationally, to this book. Wherever we teach, we are increasingly impressed with both the severity and similarity of the needs. Although our schools are increasingly challenged to meet the needs of our society, we believe they have a major influence on the way generations are learning to cooperate, collaborate, and compete.

Don Dinkmeyer, Jr., Ph.D.
LPCC, NCC
Professor, Counseling Programs
Western Kentucky University

Jon Carlson, Psy.D., Ed.D.
Distinguished Professor
Governors State University
Lake Geneva Wellness Clinic

ACKNOWLEDGMENTS

We are grateful to the graduate students in the CNS 551 Classroom Guidance graduate class at Western Kentucky University, Bowling Green, Kentucky. Their genuine examples and suggestions have helped shape this work. Thanks are also expressed to Deborah and Stephanie Dinkmeyer for their help on this project.

A special thanks to Dr. George Zimmar and the staff at Routledge for supporting this project. We are indebted to Jon Tullos and the Communications Services Department at Governors State University for the videos, which bring the concepts to life for the reader and viewer of this work.

1

INTRODUCTION AND OVERVIEW

In this chapter you will learn:

- how changes in society and school make consultation essential
- how we learn and why that is important
- the importance of self-esteem
- the three components of consulting
- guidelines for and effectiveness of consulting in schools

A shift from working directly with individuals to consultation has taken place in schools. Direct intervention with students is often a luxury that research and budgets may not support. Consulting has now become the treatment of choice for school counselors and psychologists. It has been deemed important and effective by both the American School Counselor Association (ASCA) and the National Association of School Psychologists (NASP).

We wrote *Consulting: Facilitating Human Potential and Change Processes* (Dinkmeyer & Carlson) in 1973. Much has changed in the past four decades. When the second version, *Consultation: School Mental Health Professionals as Consultants* (Dinkmeyer, Carlson, & Dinkmeyer, 1994), was published, consultation was becoming part of a class in counselor's training curriculum, convention presentations, journal articles, and Continuing Education Unit (CEU) workshops. Research studies have continued (for over 30 years) to show the power of effective consulting, but despite this history, counselors still do not often use these consultation strategies.

Our ideas have been used in U.S. schools since 1967. The approach is skill based, with its roots in Adlerian or Individual Psychology. Adlerian psychology is a goal-directed approach that emphasizes that people have choices and that therapy interventions need to build on individuals' strengths. This approach is holistic and focuses upon the total system or milieu. Our ideas have influenced millions of parents through educational programs such as Systematic Training for Effective Parenting (Dinkmeyer, McKay, & Dinkmeyer, 1998b), teachers through Systematic Training for Effective Teaching (Dinkmeyer, McKay, & Dinkmeyer, 1980), and elementary school children through Developing an Understanding of Self and Others (Dinkmeyer & Dinkmeyer, 1982).

FIVE SPECIFIC FOUNDATIONS

In this book, five assumptions are made:

1. The consultant in a school is often the school counselor.
2. Every consultant has a specific, personal set of beliefs about human behavior.
3. An effective consultation theory is necessary and adds to the personal beliefs.
4. Consultants must be able to create specific practical consultation strategies.
5. Examining case studies and commentary can increase your consulting skills.

The Consultant Is Often a School Counselor

Although others will benefit from this book, we assume school counselors comprise the baseline consultation profession in schools. School counselors have definite advantages and disadvantages when consulting in the schools, which we shall discuss. Other professions also may be consultants — school psychologists, social workers, special education teachers, and practicum students, for example. This book is equally appropriate for these individuals. The school counselor's role as a consultant, regardless of job title, is presented in Chapter 2.

Every Consultant Has a Specific Set of Beliefs about Human Behavior

Your personal beliefs about behavior have a strong influence on your consulting ability. The key to effective consultation is practical understanding of behavior, motivation, and discipline. You may, as a result of this book, expand your beliefs, change some of your beliefs, and, thereby, increase your effectiveness.

An Effective Consultation Theory Is Necessary

Our theoretical approach, based on Individual Psychology is presented in Chapter 3. The Adlerian approach complements and integrates most other theories of consultation.

Consultants Must Be Able to Tailor Strategies

The ability to create or "tailor" strategies to specific situations is the hallmark of effective consulting. Your broad knowledge base is used for different populations, hence the need for unique strategies. Consulting with teachers is different from parent consultations. Specific techniques for working with teachers, students, and parents are presented in Chapters 4 through 7.

Case Studies and Commentary Can Increase Your Consulting Skills

Consultation examples are presented. These realistic, contemporary examples show how we can change behavior when the consultation model is applied. A DVD is included with this text that allows the reader to observe us in genuine consulting sessions.

SOCIETY HAS CHANGED

Consultants need to operate systematically. The environmental and societal influences on teachers, parents, administrators, and students continue to evolve. Society continues to change, and though many changes seem beneficial, they often have a tendency to dehumanize people. In this section we will look at how society has changed, the importance of meaningful learning, and how self-esteem is a key ingredient in learning and growing.

Schools do not operate in a vacuum. They reflect America's efforts in the 21st century to prepare future adults. Therefore, to examine recent changes in our society is significant and relevant. Fundamental, substantial changes shifted our society. Passive acceptance of autocratic procedures and unequal treatment of women, minorities, and children are almost extinct. In the classroom, autocratic procedures are less effective. Students challenge demands for compliance, while techniques that encourage cooperation are increasingly effective.

A profoundly simple societal change has occurred. In the 1950s, our society was autocratic. A few people were in charge and all others were expected to obey. In the family, fathers were most often in charge. In schools, the teacher was in control of the classroom. But the pendulum swung to the other extreme. Permissiveness or chaotic relationships replaced autocratic relationships. Society shifted from an autocracy to a permissive orientation as women, minorities, and others asserted their rights. The autocrats lost control. In the family, parents tried to give their children "everything we didn't have as kids." This often meant material possessions. Although these "good" parents were well meaning, their efforts often created more harm than responsible growth. Many of these solutions are short-term satisfying and long-term unhealthy. In today's drive-through, fast-paced society, we rarely look at the longer-term implications of our actions.

The permissive society did not solve problems. In fact, it created new ones. It confused equality with entitlement. The shift in parent–child and teacher–student relationships can be illustrated: when an adult said, "Jump," the child would say, "How high?" In today's society, when an adult says, "Jump," the child says, "Why?"

We do not advocate autocratic or permissive relationships. Democratic relationships are more effective. (Although there is increasing use of the term "authoritative" to describe democratic relationships, we choose to use the term democratic. There is no political connotation to the use of the term in this text.) In democratic relationships, children are taught both freedom and responsibility. Many are confused about the meaning of "democracy." The phrase "not that you get your way, but that you have a say" may be helpful in describing a child's contribution to a democratic classroom or family. In a democratic relationship, someone is in charge. The person in charge guides others through choice making and encouragement. Consultants want to be aware of this process in order to bring about change in themselves and to guide others in order to create a democratic system.

Children do not learn about democracy vicariously; they must live it. Similarly, teachers cannot practice democracy in the classroom if they fear autocratic supervisors who are not trained in group procedures that enable them to provide democratic leadership, or if they have unequal relationships. As we shall see in later chapters, teachers will not move toward democratic classrooms if they confuse "democracy" with "chaos"; or, if they do not believe they can improve their classroom atmosphere. For most teachers in the 21st century, the keyword in their search for answers is accountability or improved performance, not "equality." Greater accountability and increased academic performance came from empowered students and teachers.

Schools are placing more demands on staff and students than ever before as curricula and knowledge bases grow. The increase in knowledge, however, is not always accompanied by commensurate increases in learning enthusiasm, or in the ability to see how the knowledge can be used or processed in daily life. This lack of inclusion or empowerment makes it far more difficult to reach performance goals.

A close inspection of educational practices and methods indicates a great disparity between the objectives and accomplishments. Unlike business, which fires the unsuccessful salesperson, schools believe that when the teacher does not "sell" or motivate the child, the child is the failure. We believe the teacher's responsibility is to teach and to take responsibility for helping each individual to learn. Most children seem to follow a prescribed path, while others need individually guided instruction. In reality, each child decides where to fit in the classroom. Children are never failures, and therefore educators must take responsibility for their schools' learning atmosphere.

IS THE PRIORITY CONTROL?

The single most important characteristic that our schools often have in common is a preoccupation with order and control. Teachers become disciplinarians with a goal of the absence of noise and movement. Children sitting silently and motionless is unnatural and unlikely. Schools also assume that all students will be interested in the same topic at the same moment for the same length of time. Educators often expect virtually perfect copies of the "ideal" student. Teachers smile in recognition at the well-worn phrase "Don't let them see you smile until October." Although most teachers do not act this way, some believe its underlying assumption.

Our economic and political systems appear to reward material gains. Social responsibility, spiritual values, and character are discussed and verbally lauded, but they are seldom prized and rewarded. Additionally, teachers and parents do not model what they preach (Dinkmeyer et al., 1998a). Individuals are engaged in talking about equality while demonstrating inequality at all levels. The administrator feels superior to the teacher, the teacher feels superior to the parent, the parent feels superior to the child, and the child struggles to get "rights." From this struggle emerges the "getting" person, one concerned about what he or she can accomplish for self. The result is that we are becoming more selfish and remaining unconcerned for others.

Schools are often more concerned with preparing for annual spring achievement tests. This is important, and so is cooperation, but rarely if ever is a connection made to success through authoritative leadership. In fact, successful learning is best accomplished in an underlying atmosphere that includes a cooperative relationship between teacher and student. In practice, our goals and objectives appear to be limited to acquiring facts. We tell children that democracy, cooperation, peace, and brotherhood are the goals of a happy and successful life. Yet, we introduce, train for, and demonstrate these concepts in an authoritarian and competitive manner — the direct opposite of the stated objectives. Students learn from what we do rather than from what we say. The model of the benevolent autocrat who fosters competition is internalized.

To meet the challenge of our times we must live truly as equals. This ideal recognizes that we are equal in value even though we might not be equal in social position. The basic social conflict involves a struggle for control, the overambition to be more than others, and the resultant nagging feeling of inadequacy and alienation. The challenge is clear: We must learn to live as equals. Equality does not mean equal intelligence, responsibility, or commitment. It means the ability to treat one another with mutual respect. This goal is best accomplished in a democratic, firm, and fair atmosphere.

Consultants must become familiar with democratic procedures. The democratic system is often new to consultants. Therefore, we have people attempting to operate a system who have not experienced a functional democracy. Their experiences with people at home and at school were superior–inferior relationships. Democratic procedures require that each person must choose and become responsible for his or her own behavior, and as a result be self-reliant. There is still a need for someone to take control and be in charge.

THE IMPORTANCE OF THE SYSTEM

The school of human behavior, which had its origins in the work of Sigmund Freud, concentrated on the individual and the intrapersonal. In contrast, Alfred Adler stressed the importance of the context, environment, and system in which the individual lives, as well as the interpersonal. The emergence of family systems theory has validated Adler's ideas. This approach holds that if an individual has problems it is because the social system is unhealthy or disturbed. The sick or troubled individual is actually viewed as the "identified patient" from the system.

How does this relate to schools? Students with problems need to be viewed as living with "sick" or dysfunctional families and classrooms. When interventions focus on changing the system through work with parents, teachers, administrators, and the curriculum, dysfunctional behavior is reduced. Healthy systems are those that allow all members to belong with positive and constructive places, and they in turn have or create methods of effective problem solving.

Consultants need to view their clients within the larger systems in which the clients reside. They begin by asking questions like: What is wrong with the system? What needs to be improved? What is oppressive? or How is the negative behavior being maintained? rather than What is wrong with this student?

THE IMPORTANCE OF LEARNING

Two components of learning are information and meaning. When we fail to learn, it is because we have not discovered the meaning of the information we have. Nothing is learned until it has become personally meaningful. Then it influences our perceptions and behavior. We know we should listen to feelings and beliefs of our students, but we have so many "pages to cover."

Teachers do not fail because they do not know their subject matter. They fail because they are unable to make this information meaningful. The information component of the learning process lies outside the learner. The meaning aspect lies within the learner. Educators often want to change learning by altering the information component. This paradox is rarely discussed, much less understood, by educators.

The rationale follows these lines: If a little information is a good thing, then a whole lot must be a whole lot better. Subsequently, we may be drowning students in information with the following approaches:

- longer days and longer semesters at school
- more academic courses
- less physical education or anything considered a frill, such as music, drama, or art

Most of us do not need more information. More important than the giving of information is helping people understand the personal meaning of the information. Take dropouts, drug abusers, or school failures for example. They did not drop out because of a lack of information. They were not, however, helped to see the relationship between the information and their personal needs. Involvement and meaning were not developed. A big difference exists between knowing and behaving. Knowing results from acquiring new information. A change in behavior comes with the discovery of meaning.

Students need to feel safe and secure before they can feel challenged. If they are not safe, they feel threatened. Threat deters learning, while challenge fosters learning. Yet we continue to threaten children in order to motivate (e.g., grades, no recess, "I'll send a note home").

The evolution of an effective consultation process may require changes as radical as the technological shifts of the past decade. These changes will require boldness, imagination, and hard work. Change requires optimism and a belief in the intrinsic worth of each person. Change requires changing the people who set the policy, make the decisions, and facilitate the growth of students. This change can occur only by dealing with the person's beliefs.

Education should prepare people not just to make or earn a living, but to live creative, humane, and sensitive lives. The purpose of education is to educate educators to turn out men and women who are capable of educating their friends, their communities, and most important, themselves. Education is not a spectator sport. It is life, and each individual needs to get involved. The problem is larger, as Rudolf Dreikurs (1971) indicated when he stated:

> Today husband and wife cannot live separately with each other if they do not treat each other as equals. Nor can parents get along with their children if they assume that children can be subdued. There can be no harmony and stability in the community unless each member of it has his safe place as an equal to all others. There can be no cooperation between management and labor unless each group feels respected and trusted by the other. There can be no peace on earth unless one nation respects the rights and dignity of another. (p. xiii)

The lack of change and quality of "sameness" in our schools is illustrated in one of the few video tapes that captured Dreikurs. He listens as teachers share concerns about the challenges of teachers, who state: "We have to compete with the media." "They expect us to be entertainers." "Formerly students complied, now they challenge." These comments were made more than 30 years ago. Hairstyles and fashion have changed, but the challenges spoken by the teachers of the 1960s are equally appropriate today.

SELF-ESTEEM

Self-esteem, believing you are of value, is a key trait in successful living. A number of factors in schools have a negative influence upon self-esteem. As one passes through school, an increasing emphasis is placed upon memorizing (despite teachers professing to reinforce creative, curious, and spontaneous children) if one is to achieve the typical rewards of the school.

Schools also discourage students from developing the capacity to learn by and for themselves because schools are structured in a way as to make students dependent upon teachers. Students' curiosity, spontaneity, and courage are not reinforced. Their ability and desire to think and act for themselves are diminished rather than increased.

A stated educational goal is to help children develop responsibility for the direction of their lives. In our society, we do not let children assume responsibility for their futures until they reach the late teenage years. At that time they are expected to make reasonable decisions and choices. Yet prior to this time, they have had little training and no experience in decision making, often having parents that still wake them up in the morning, remind them to do their homework, and provide other unnecessary services; thus, the resulting high dropout rate and high divorce rate. This suggests education and education for life are a random series of events that guarantee equal doses of failure and success.

A child cannot become a successful learner only through the experiences of others. In order to become successful, one must experience success. The student must get involved, including the ability to evaluate his or her performance.

Technology has had a tremendous impact upon U.S. education. The launching of the Russian *Sputnik* in 1957 is recognized as the time when the United States first felt challenged by the scientific achievement of other cultures. As this effort continued through the 1960s, emphasis on science, math, and other academic subjects conformed. What became increasingly apparent was that a greater amount of information was available than one could readily master through traditional methods. Thus, U.S. education providers had to decide whether we should emphasize facts and information or, instead, attitudes.

The decision was made to place an emphasis on acquiring knowledge. This resulted in placing college subjects in the high school curricula and moving high school subjects to the elementary level. One might only speculate on the results if instead we had focused on developing positive attitudes toward learning and a desire to become involved in the educational process as a lifetime task.

In response to the Soviet threat, the National Defense Education Act (NDEA) poured millions of dollars into the schools. In fact, the elementary school counseling profession was created through NDEA. Teachers were paid stipends to increase their teaching skills. In some cases, teachers were also paid to train as school counselors. If education is to stress humaneness, there must be a systematic emphasis in the following areas:

1. New life patterns emerging in response to changing knowledge and technology will require schools and colleges to function decreasingly as primary sources of knowledge and increasingly as developers of capacities to process information and reorganize experiences obtained in family, community, work situations, and a variety of complementary institutions.

2. Vigorous measures are needed to strengthen the knowledge base from which education operates. The emphasis needs to be on making current information meaningful rather than on giving more information.

3. Greatly increased effort must be directed toward establishing the essential preconditions for effective learning.

4. Continuous curriculum adaptation is necessary in order to receive new inputs which reflect (a) the current state of knowledge in each subject of instruction, and (b) the behavioral knowledge applicable to teaching and learning.

5. Education needs better processes for helping individuals order their values so as to help them make better choices as to how their energies and eventually their lives are spent.

6. New skills in the workplace must include exploring alternatives, making successful transitions, and the ability to function in a democratic environment.

WHY CONSULTATION?

The need for counselors to be skilled in consultation has been clearly articulated (Brown, Spano, & Schulte, 1988; Nelson & Shifron, 1985; Umansky & Holloway, 1984), and the counseling profession has responded. The Council for Accreditation of Counseling and Related Educational Programs (CACREP, 2001) includes a requirement for curricular experience in the theories and applications of consultation in its standards for accreditation for graduate programs; and the American School Counselor Association (2004) has included consultation in its national model for school counseling programs. The Association for Counselor Education and Supervision has published two handbooks on consultation (Brown, Kurpius, & Morris, 1988; Kurpius & Brown, 1988). Although it is deemed critical that counseling students receive training in consultation, research suggests that many counselor education programs provide only minimal education in this area, and that students are graduating without proper preparation in consultation (Brown, Kurpius, & Morris, 1988). Innovative strategies to convey the basic principles and techniques of consultation are needed.

Consultation offers counselors a powerful tool to change the school environment and community. Reynolds et al. (1984) summarized the literature that compared the effectiveness of consulting with that of counseling. The research supported the fact that consulting was much more time efficient and therefore cost effective. The counselor who works with one client impacts one person and his or her life. The consultant who works with one teacher indirectly affects the lives of 30 or more children. The consultant who works with one parent education group may affect the lives of 20 to 30 children.

With this rationale in mind we have selected to work with those who have the largest impact on the school system: teachers, parents, and administrators. Additionally, if the parent or teacher changes, then changing the student is easier. Often students have little motivation to change on their own.

Counselors are able to help students to function more effectively in their environment, while consultants are more likely to change the environment. Parents are taught to teach their children social skills and to create home environments where children can flourish socially, emotionally, and intellectually. Teachers can learn to create a similar environment, and administrators are helped to develop a system where human needs are of the highest priority.

According to Brown, Kurpius, and Morris (1988), through consultation, primary prevention programs can be developed that will contribute to work, family, and educational environments that will be less likely to contribute to dysfunctional living. Parents who learn to deal with an underachieving child may be better able to prevent that syndrome in the future with their other children. Employers who inadvertently create stressful environments may be able to increase commitment, reduce absenteeism and tardiness, and reduce health care costs, simply by restructuring the workplace. Consultants have helped teachers, parents, employees, and others become effective agents against mental health problems.

CONSULTATION DEFINED

Each consultation has three parties: the consultant, the consultee, and the client or problem. In Figure 1.1 the three parties and the flow (relationship) between them are displayed. However, a consultant can be any individual asked to intervene in a situation in which a consultee

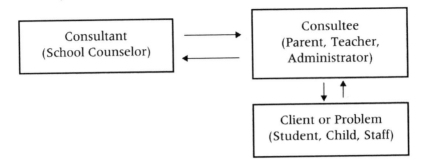

Fig. 1.1 The consultation process. The consultant, the consultee, and the child or problem and the relationship.

and a problem exist. Consultants are skilled at understanding consultees and their problems.

The consultee typically brings the problem to the first meeting. Consultees are often teachers, parents, or administrators. The consultee's problem may be either a person or a situation, sometimes both. For example, a teacher may find a specific student to be the problem; a principal's problem might be a lack of discipline in most classrooms. Most consultation situations involve adults attempting to change adult–student relationships. Students are not directly involved in the consultation.

Consultation involves sharing information, observing, providing a sounding board, and developing tentative hypotheses for action. The emphasis is on equal relationships developed through collaboration and joint planning. The purpose is to develop tentative recommendations that fit the uniqueness of the child, the teacher, the parent, and the setting. The consultant is not the problem-solving expert.

Consultation relationships have the following four characteristics:

1. Information, observations, and concerns about a problem are shared between the consultant and the consultee.
2. Tentative hypotheses are developed to assess the situation.
3. Joint planning and collaboration occurs between consultant and consultee.
4. The hypotheses, or recommendations, reflect and respect the uniqueness of the child, the teacher, and the setting.

These four points emphasize the equality of the relationship between the consultee and consultant. A widespread faulty belief about school consultation relationships is that teachers send students to consultants to be "fixed." This is not a consultation relationship.

SHARING INFORMATION

The school consultant is able to bring new ideas to the consultee. Equally important, the consultant helps the consultee assess a personal solution. The consultant teaches the consultee skills and a systematic approach for solving similar problems in the future. Information concerning behavior, misbehavior, group dynamics, teachers' beliefs, discipline procedures, and motivation techniques are all part of the consultant's repertoire. In Chapter 4 we present this information and make suggestions on the most appropriate teaching methods in the consultation relationship.

The primary characteristic of the consultant's repertoire is that it is consistent with a theory of human behavior that the consultant thinks will help the consultee. We can summarize our approach by stating that all behavior, even misbehavior, has a purpose that can be understood. Further, the most effective techniques for change require the consultee, the person most interested in change, to initiate new behaviors.

PROVIDING A SOUNDING BOARD

Most consultants have been trained in counseling and listening skills. When the consultee presents a situation, that effective listening must precede any new information. Effective consultants must be capable of focused reflective listening. This is a cornerstone skill in counseling that is equally important in consultation. Ivey and Ivey (2004) call this "hearing the client's story." If we structure our consultation on this construct, the story gives us clues toward purpose, strengths, and beliefs. Additionally, the consultant goes beyond listening and facilitates understanding of the dynamics of behavior through effective questions. We have found that well-chosen questions lead to effective information gathering.

MAINTAINING AN EQUAL RELATIONSHIP

A superior-to-inferior relationship suggests that consultees seek advice that consultants dispense. Instead, we advocate an equal relationship. Equality means the consultant is not an expert dispensing advice on demand. The consultee has equal responsibility for changing the situation, which prompts the consultation relationship. This perspective on the consulting relationship is different from traditional, widespread beliefs about the consultant's role in schools.

CHANGING BOTH BELIEFS AND BEHAVIOR

Consultants realize that unless concrete action takes place as a result of the consultation meeting, nothing has changed. The consultant operates not as an expert suggestion dispenser, but rather as a facilitator who helps the consultee to develop workable recommendations. The consultant need not feel totally comfortable or committed about the recommendations the consultee develops. Recommendations come not only from the consultant, but also from the consultee. Recommendations are not just about behavior, but they also deal specifically with the beliefs of the consultee. Beliefs "fuel" or drive behaviors.

INEFFECTIVE ROLES VERSUS EFFECTIVE ROLES

The consultant's role needs to be clearly understood by teachers, parents, and administrators. These stakeholders must be educated as to how this role differs from traditional counseling roles. Defining consultation as only responding to requests from teachers, administrators, and parents may create ineffective consultation relationships. Effective consultation is not simply responding to a sometimes confusing and demanding set of requests. Consider the following examples:

Mrs. Page, a third-grade teacher, frequently sends students to the counselor. She reports the students are disrupting the classroom and would benefit from special attention by the counselor.

The principal asks the counselor to become part of the school's discipline system. Any student sent to the office twice in one week must see the counselor.

The mother of a fifth grader is concerned her son will be asked to repeat that grade unless he shows improvement. Can the counselor talk to the teacher, or principal, or both?

These three situations could easily become ineffective consultation situations. The consultant must understand the underlying belief each person has about the nature of change. In each of these situations, the person (consultee) believes the counselor (consultant) will solve the problem. Perhaps the most widespread and difficult problem-solving belief is that the consultant can "fix the child."

PROBLEM OWNERSHIP

Consultants understand the importance of problem ownership. If a consultee comes to the consultant with a problem, the consultee owns the problem. Who owns the problem often guides the next steps in a consultation.

In the previous example with Mrs. Page, the consultant would need to work with Mrs. Page and help her understand how the children are a problem for *her* and what *she* might do differently. The principal in the previous example needs to understand how discipline is the responsibility of the teacher or administrator in charge, and that to take the student out of the situation to talk with the counselor does little to change the existing system. Finally, with the concerned mother, the consultant needs to help her learn how to deal effectively with her child and the significant adults in her child's world. This includes making good decisions for the welfare of her child.

Counselors are often given lists of referred students. The referring teachers are generally friendly and cooperative, as they expect you, the consultant, to solve their problem. The counselor is expected to help the student who often does not see the problem or feel a need to change. Without the involvement of the referring teacher, the counselor (and the student) are at a big disadvantage.

However, by working with the referring teacher, the consultant can become effective. The teacher is upset and in a state of dissonance. He or she has a problem and wants it solved. By helping the teacher to own the problem and take responsibility for its resolution, the disadvantage is gone. *The one who wants change can create it.* The one who needs help will get it, and the one who wants the help is able to help him- or herself.

School counselors are not serving as consultants when they act as a referral service for misbehaving students. Unless the teacher is equally involved in the process, the process is not consultation. Recent writers in the field of consultation seem to show clearly how consultation works in the school setting. However, no one broad or universally accepted definition of consultation has been accepted (Brown, Kurpius, & Morris, 1988; Dougherty, 2005; Hansen, Himes, & Meier, 1990).

CONSULTATION: A BRIEF HISTORY

The setting for consultation began in hospitals and mental health clinics where medical personnel asked for additional services to solve medical diagnoses. This approach, asking for help to solve problems, spread to industry, community agencies, and schools.

The role of a consultant depends on the services provided. Schein (1969) described an "expert" consultation role in which the consultant solves the problems. For example, the patient with a skin condition is referred to a dermatologist because the family physician cannot diagnose the condition. The dermatologist (the consultant) identifies the condition and prescribes the remedy.

Another consultation role more closely identified with school counselors is the prescriptive mode. The consultant gathers information and identifies the problem and then tells the consultee what steps should be taken (Kurpius & Brubaker, 1976). The role resembles that of the medical doctor because the consultant unilaterally reaches the conclusion/solution and then offers it to the consultee.

The role that most clearly resembles ours is that of a collaborator, one who forms relationships with the consultees in order to help them change. In this relationship, a joint diagnosis occurs with a focus on helping consultees to develop their own solutions. The consultant serves as a facilitator of the problem-solving process. This role allows the consultee to develop skills and enables him or her to not depend on the consultant.

Dougherty (2005) placed the origin of today's counselor and consultant with the school psychologists of the 1920s. Events in the 1950s moved schools closer to the ideals of the present. The 1954 Thayer Conference was a major precursor for the present day NASP. In 1957, the Soviet Union launched *Sputnik*, a basketball-sized object destined to launch the modern space race. Massive amounts of funding were then poured into U.S. education. The purpose, in simple terms, was to create more and better scientists to launch more and better satellites.

The NDEA of 1958 served as the conduit for this funding. Not since 1862, when an act of Congress created land-grant universities, had society poured so much money and effort into education. A new profession was created — elementary school counselor.

These counselors were free of historical constraints. No need for college advising or testing meant time to focus on classroom dynamics. A journal for elementary counselors was created in 1963, and soon articles describing consultations with teachers and parents were published. By 1968, 12 articles on consultants had been written in all journals.

A 1966 report by members of the school counseling and counselor education professors made consultation an "official" school counselor role. In 1973, the first edition of this text was published, one of the first dedicated solely to the idea of consultation in the schools (Dinkmeyer & Carlson, 1973).

Legislation enacted in 1975 made consultation with special needs students and parents an integral part of the mainstream. PL94-142 is synonymous with the efforts schools make to help special needs students. This movement continues; the legislation is now more commonly referred to as the Individuals with Disabilities Education Act (IDEA).

THE NEED TO CREATE CONSULTATION PRIORITIES

Effective consultation works with teachers, parents, administrators, curriculum, and the classroom rather than directly with the individual. Consultants need to be clear and let others know exactly what they do. We believe that each school and community will dictate the exact priorities. For every population, the consultant emphasizes the opportunity to teach and educate. The following are some possible changes:

- Training teachers in the skills of effective teaching (i.e., motivation, discipline, working in groups, communication)
- Training parents in the skills of effective parenting (i.e., goals of misbehavior, motivation, communication, discipline, family meetings)
- Weekly teacher problem-solving groups (or C groups) to help deal with the normal problems parents face
- Individual meetings with teachers and parents to help them with their problems and concerns with specific children
- Individual meetings with administrators to help them with their ongoing problems
- Create curricula to help children learn the necessary life skills (i.e., problem solving, goal setting, values clarification, self-discipline, self-motivation)

Consultants frequently complain that the people who need help won't get it. It is helpful to not get discouraged with this situation. Take a lesson from the medical community, which uses the process of triage. Triage calls for dividing casualties into three groups: mildly wounded, moderately wounded, and mortally wounded. Work with the mildly wounded so that they won't become more seriously infected. If we spend all our time with those who are "mortally wounded" and cannot be helped, we will quickly become discouraged. Begin by working with those people who want help.

TECHNOLOGY CREATES OPPORTUNITY

This text incorporates a DVD. Its purpose is to illustrate teacher and parent consultation in realistic situations. Six examples allow readers to integrate ideas into practice. Ten years ago, such technology was simply impossible.

Electronic mail (e-mail) has, in many cases, replaced phone, face-to-face, or paper communication between school stakeholders. Does e-mail hold potential for the consultant? Kruger et al. (2001) conducted a study that showed that using e-mail reduced teachers' feelings of isolation and enhanced teacher knowledge. Multiple emerging techno-logies can enhance our learning process.

SUMMARY

The consultant utilizes skills in interpersonal relationships, learning processes, and group procedures to facilitate the development of the helping relationship between staff members and students. This book presents a theory of human behavior, which is designed to facilitate more effective human relationships. It includes a theoretical rationale for the consultant as a specialist in human relationships; the theory and practice of consulting with teachers, administrators, and parents; and practical examples of work with individuals and groups. The classroom as well as the system as a whole are discussed, and methods for releasing their inherent human potential are presented.

REVIEW QUESTIONS

1. How have changes from autocratic to democratic living affected society in general and schools specifically?
2. What are the characteristics of a democratic relationship?
3. Do you believe people can really live as equals?
4. How can consultants help teachers learn to make learning more meaningful?
5. Describe how schools discourage students and create low self-esteem.
6. What is meant by humaneness, and how can schools really create humane environments?
7. How would you develop a rationale for consulting in the schools? Include your priorities.
8. What are the four characteristics of a consultation relationship?
9. How would you define consultation?

REFERENCES

American School Counselor Association. (2004). *The ASCA national model: A framework for school counseling programs.* Alexandria, VA: Author.

Brown, D., Kurpius, D. J., & Morris, J. R. (1988). *Handbook of consultation with individuals and small groups.* Alexandria, VA: Association for Counselor Education and Supervision.

Brown, D., Spano, D. B., & Schulte, A. C. (1988). Consultation training in master's level counselor education programs. *Counselor Education and Supervision, 27,* 323–330.

Council for Accreditation of Counseling and Related Educational Programs. (2001). *Accreditation standards of the Council for Accreditation of Counseling and Related Educational Programs.* Alexandria, VA: Author.

Dinkmeyer, D., & Carlson, J. (1973). *Consulting: Facilitating human potential and change processes.* Columbus, OH: Charles Merrill.

Dinkmeyer, D., Carlson, J., & Dinkmeyer, D., Sr. (1994). *Consultation: School mental health professional as consultants.* Muncie, IN: Accelerated Development.

Dinkmeyer, D., & Dinkmeyer, D., Jr. (1982). *DUSO (Developing understanding of self and others). I and II.* Circle Pines, MN: American Guidance Service.

Dinkmeyer, D., McKay, G. & Dinkmeyer, D., Jr. (1998c). *STEP (Systematic training for effective parenting).* Circle Pines, MN: American Guidance Service.

Dinkmeyer, D., McKay, G., & Dinkmeyer, D., Jr. (1980). *STET (Systematic training for effective teaching).* Circle Pines, MN: American Guidance Service.

Dinkmeyer, D., McKay, G., & Dinkmeyer, J. (1998b). *Early childhood STEP.* Circle Pines. MN: American Guidance Service.

Dinkmeyer, D., McKay, G., & Dinkmeyer, D., Jr. (1998a). *STEP/Teen (Systematic training for effective parenting of teenagers).* Circle Pines, MN: American Guidance Service.

Dougherty, A. (2005). *Psychological consultation and collaboration in school and community settings.* Belmont, CA: Thomson, Brooks/Cole.

Dreikurs, R., Grunwald, B., & Pepper, F. (1971) *Maintaining sanity in the classroom.* New York: Harper and Row.

Hansen, J. C., Himes, B. S., & Meier, S. (1990). *Consultation: Concepts and practices.* Englewood Cliffs, NJ: Prentice-Hall.

Ivey, A., & Ivey, M. (2004). Intentional interviewing: Facilitating climate development in a multicultural society (5th ed). Belmont, CA: Thomson, Brooks/Cole.

Kruger, L., Struzziero, J., Kaplan, S., Macklem, G., Watts. R., & Weksel, T. (2001). The use of e-mail in consultation: An exploratory study of consultee outcomes. *Journal of Educational and Psychological Consultation, 12*(2), 133–149.

Kurpius, D. J., & Brown, D. (1988). *Handbook of consultation: An intervention for advocacy and outreach.* Alexandria, VA: Association for Counselor Education and Supervision.

Kurpius, D. J., & Brubaker, J. C. (1976). *Psycho-educational consultation: Definition — function — preparation.* Bloomington: Indiana University Press.

Nelson, R. C., & Shifron, R. (1985). Choice awareness in consultation. *Counselor Education and Supervision, 24,* 298–306.

Reynolds, C. R., Gutkin, T. B., Elliot, S. N., & Witt, J. C. (1984). *School psychology: Essentials of theory and practice.* New York: Wiley.

Schein, E. H. (1969). *Process consultation: Its role in organization development.* Reading, MA: Addison-Wesley.

Umansky, D. L., & Holloway, E. L. (1984). The counselor as consultant: From model lo practice. *School Counselor, 32,* 329–338.

2

THE CONSULTANT'S ROLE

In this chapter, you will learn:

- traditional expectations for school counselors
- alternatives to these traditional expectations
- the importance of communication skills
- the importance of primary prevention

HUMAN POTENTIAL

School has an influence on each child's self-perception, or self-esteem. As early as 1963, research suggested that a student's self-esteem decreases as the child continues in school (Combs & Soper, 1963). The topic continues to fuel research across the decades. Wiggins and Schatz (1994) refer to studies such as Bloom (1977), Clemes and Bean (1981), and Wiggins (1987) as empirical evidence of the importance of self-esteem to school achievement.

Does self-esteem change as a student moves through the school system? This can be anecdotally "proven" by thinking about the "average attitude" of two grade levels: first and 11th. Usually, with a decade of schooling under their belts, many high school students do not have high self-esteem. Sometimes they no longer choose to participate in the institution, adding to the dropout rate. The school experience either builds or erodes self-esteem. In the elementary school, a child's lifestyle, the basic set of beliefs about self and others, is established. Often this lifestyle is established by the second grade.

Even the terminology — self-esteem versus self-concept — can be confusing or contradictory. King (1994) thoroughly discusses this topic while pointing out the inherent importance of the ideas to education. Self-concept can be defined as the perception one has about him- or herself; self-esteem can be defined as the extent to which one is satisfied with this perception. For example, a student's self-concept may be: "I am not very smart" and his or her self-esteem in this area may be: "But that's okay because I am capable in other areas." The California Task Force to Promote Self-Esteem (California Department of Education, 1990) defined it as "appreciating my own worth and importance ... having the character to be accountable for myself and to act responsibly towards others."

The connection between self-esteem and academic ability or performance is a major area of interest. Moeller (1994) summarizes the state of the research as:

> Research consistently indicates that children's self-concept seems to be determined, at least in part, by their academic performance, especially in early elementary years. It thus seems especially important to help children do well academically during those years, since academic self-concept might be causally related to academic performance in middle and high school. (p. 3)

Studies on self-esteem continue to interest researchers. A study in the United Kingdom found academic self-esteem and a movement away from academics from those not capable of strong performance. Humphrey, Charlton, and Newton (2004) suggest this may account for part of the adolescent "scholastic counter-culture," with the equivalent of seventh grade or age 12 as a particularly critical period of perceptual reorganization for low achievers.

The elementary school years profoundly affect the educational development of children. When consultants understand the interdependence of the affective (self-concept) and cognitive areas of learning, positive influences can be initiated. Our approach to this critical area is presented in two extensive educational programs (Dinkmeyer & Dinkmeyer, 1982a, 1982b). This approach is presented in Chapter 6.

CONSULTANT CHARACTERISTICS

An informal survey for the Association for Counselor Education and Supervision (ACES) Task Force on Consultation provides an interesting insight into perceptions of effective consultants. The survey asked one question: "Please list the three most important characteristics, skills, or capabilities you would desire in a consultant hired to provide assistance to you on your job." The 49 elementary and middle school teachers responding to this question indicated six major characteristics as listed in Table 2.1.

Many of these characteristics are consistent with our definition of effective consultation presented in Chapter 1. When consultants are effective, they share specific knowledge and skills, which they then can share with the consultee.

Consultants Work With People

Consultants work with specific clients. The consultee (client) will bring a challenge related to their work setting. In schools, most often this is a teacher presenting a problem with a student or group of students. While the consultant and consultee work together, the consultant often becomes a teacher to the teacher. This means the consultant understands the dynamics of the consultation challenge, can clearly articulate it to the consultee, and is able to give the consultee new ideas on how to handle the challenge. The relationship is intended to be temporary; one session or more, but always with an endpoint or goal driving the relationship. It is remedial; the consultee is attempting to correct an unsatisfactory situation.

We refer to the consultation model as "triadic." This means there is always a third party, rarely present, who is directly affected by the consultation. Finally, the consultant can be external or internal to the school system. An internal consultant would be the school counselor assigned to the school, for example an external consultant, a specialist (even a counselor), who is responsible for several schools.

TABLE 2.1 Consultant Characteristics Desired by Elementary and Middle School Teachers

Characteristic	%
Knowledgeable	26
Communicative ability/good listener	19
Specific techniques/practical approach	11
Expertise	8
Good personality	7
Someone who has been in classroom	6

Source: Dinkmeyer, 1987.

The Consultant as a Person

The effective consultant possesses personal qualities and abilities that enhance effectiveness as a facilitator of human potential. The consultant's training involves course work that provides a number of required group experiences that enable the consultant to become more aware of self, impact upon others, and personal values and purposes.

The consultant is expected to be competent in the following areas:

1. *Empathy and understanding of how others feel and experience their world.*
2. *Ability to relate to children and adults in a purposeful manner.* This involves the ability to establish rapport, to develop effective working relationships, and to use time in a judicious manner. Able to establish relationships with consultees; this relationship fits consultation goals.
3. *Sensitivity to human needs.* Able to perceive a need and be available as a facilitator to help the person meet that need.
4. Awareness of psychological dynamics, motivations, and purpose of human behavior.
5. *Understanding of group dynamics and its significance for the educational establishment.* The consultant is aware of the impact of group forces upon the teacher, seeing the teacher in the context of forces from without (such as administration and parents) and forces from within (such as personal goals and purposes).
6. *Capability of establishing relationships that are characterized by mutual trust and mutual respect.* A consultant to either a group or an individual should inspire confidence. Mutual respect includes the belief that consultees are collaborators.
7. *Capability of taking a risk on an important issue.* Able to take a stand on significant issues that affect human development. The consultant's role requires a courageous approach to life. This involves the "courage to be imperfect," or recognizing that mistakes may be made, but realizing mistakes are learning experiences, and one is not immobilized by the fear of making mistakes. This courage is developed through group experiences and in the supervised practical experience.
8. *Ability to establish the necessary and sufficient conditions for a helping relationship.* This is perhaps the most important quality of all. The consultant should be creative, spontaneous, and imaginative. The consultant position, by its very nature, demands flexibility and the ability to deal with a variety of

expectations — on one hand, the principal's need for order and structure; on the other, the child's need for participation, care, and concern.

9. *Capability of inspiring leadership at a number of levels.* Educational administrators often look to consultants as specialists in understanding human behavior, while parents see the consultant as a specialist in child psychology. Teachers see the consultant as a resource in correction with pupil personnel problems. Children might see consultants as a resource in helping them to understand themselves and others.

Our belief is that this type of person emerges most readily from a training program that places an emphasis upon not only the cognitive skills of the graduate student, but also upon developing an awareness of self and one's impact upon others. We believe that this type of personal development is best arranged through regularly scheduled group experiences that enable the individual to become more aware of his or her effect on colleagues. The helping profession cannot tolerate the ineffectual person, the one who is able, perhaps, to relate to children but not to adults, or vice versa. The school consultant must be capable of establishing human relationships.

These are high standards. Not all consultants will attain this level upon completion of training, and personal growth is a continual process. However, we need to recognize that these traits are not mere platitudes. Coursework alone does not develop adequate consultants. *No single factor is more destructive to consultant progress than a lack of ability to develop effective helping relationships.*

Communication in Consultation

The consultant is not only a specialist in human relationships but also in communication. Messages sent by both consultants and consultees are always multifaceted, including content and feeling. As an active and skilled listener, the consultant must hear both the words and the feelings in order to get the message from the consultee. The consultant helps the client to become a more effective listener by hearing the total message.

Some messages are incongruent. The consultant should look for words that may be different from the feeling. For example, a variety of ways exist for saying "I am happy" or "I am angry" to make feelings incongruent with the words. One must note tone of voice, facial expression, and other nonverbal clues. The consultant is aware of various methods of dealing with stress. Virginia Satir (1988) developed a classic format for analyzing the difference between manipulative and actualization response forms. The consultant's goal is to develop responses where the communication is characterized by hearing, listening, understanding, and mutual meaning.

The types of responses still relevant today include:

1. *Placating.* This style of response is used by a person who always keeps safe, attempts to placate, or be the martyr. The person crosses self out as unimportant and is willing to agree with anything the other person offers.

2. *Blaming.* This style of response is used by the person who is aggressive. This person is suspicious that others take advantage and essentially believes "Only I am important." Others don't count, so they are crossed out. This has been classified as "the boss" response.

3. *Conniving and Reasonable.* This style of response is used by communicators who put an emphasis on being correct and in not letting anyone know their weaknesses. They speak as if they were computers and have no feelings.

4. *Avoiding and Irrelevant.* This style of response is used by the person who essentially talks as if he or she has no relationship to others, almost as if he or she were "psychotic." This person says, "I am not here and you are not here." There is no attempt to communicate.

5. *Congruent.* This style of response equals real communication in which the affect and words are congruent. A person who makes a congruent response creates a relationship that is real and safe. The consultant models this level of responding as consultants and clients work toward it. (Satir, 1988)

Although many communication systems to evaluate the quality of communication have been developed since Satir's work, the underlying assumptions remain consistent. A *low-level response* does not acknowledge content. A *medium-level response* begins to understand the feeling within the statement. The *highest level response* understands both content and feeling in a way that adds to the dialogue.

Although Satir is often cited as a classic example of offering a helpful communications approach, other mental health professionals continue to expand this area. Hawes (1989) presented a method of communication training between teachers and children in which the school counselor was a consultant and trainer.

Verbal messages too often are destructive and do not facilitate growth. Communication is at times ineffective because we send ineffectual messages. Examples of these ineffective messages include procedures such as the following:

1. *Ordering and commanding* are ineffective because they deny the mutual aspect of the consultation relationship.
2. *Warning and admonishing* consultees to stop certain behaviors reflects an attitude that communicates judgment. Guilt or resentment will follow.
3. *Exhorting and moralizing* present messages such as "My way is best." They deny the right of the consultee to make decisions.
4. *Advising and providing solutions* without hearing the consultee's situation derails the consultation relationship.
5. *Lecturing* is best left for university courses. It is an ineffective consultation style.
6. *Judging and criticizing* elevate the role of the consultant so that consultant and consultee are no longer on an equal communication level.
7. *Praising and agreeing* are ineffective motivation techniques.
8. *Name calling and ridiculing* are best left for the playground.
9. *Interpreting and analyzing* should not be the beginning states of a consultation relationship.
10. *Reassuring and sympathizing* may be perceived as false. They are not effective encouragement skills.
11. *Probing, questioning, and interrogating* may be inappropriate if the consultee is not ready.
12. *Withdrawing, humoring, and diverting* do not accurately reflect the consultee's situation.

Many consultee statements may bring about ineffective communication. The consultant develops congruent communications and is alert to any ineffectual communication with the consultee. *Helping the consultee to become aware of ineffective communication patterns is an important step in the consultation relationship.*

CONSULTANT LEADS AND TRANSACTIONS

Consultation can be limited in its effectiveness if the communication skills of the consultant are poor. Confusing verbal and nonverbal messages may restrict open communication. A consultant's limited conception of the role may create the perception of an "expert" able to answer all questions. If the staff accepts the image, they present their problems.

Instead, the process must be collaborative with total involvement of the consultee for the productive hypotheses to be generated and workable corrective procedures to be established. The parable of either fishing *for* the person, or teaching him or her to fish illustrates our point. The former requires daily interaction; the latter, one lesson.

Effective consulting is tailored to the uniqueness of both the client and the consultee. This establishes communication that is open. It deals with all of the messages, especially the feelings and personal meanings within the content that are often not understood in ordinary social conversations or communications between professionals.

These procedures must go beyond telling, lecturing, advising, and sharing "opinions." In contrast, one must establish an atmosphere that encourages sharing and exploring ideas. *Effective consulting engages the cognitive and affective domains.* It seeks to examine and share ideas, openly exploring the feelings of all concerned, and to move toward commitments to action. The relationship operates on the premise that emotional communication is two-way, insofar as it elicits feedback and processes the feedback continuously to clarify the messages that are being sent and their meanings.

The essence of consultation is communication. The consultant must be able to understand the messages being sent and be sensitive to the relationship with the consultee. This necessitates being aware of one's verbal and nonverbal communication and the impressions that are being developed in the transactions with the staff.

A consultant lead is the initiation of a transaction or the response to the consultee. Consultant leads influence the responses of the consultee and may focus on:

1. Techniques that focus on content:

   - Encouraging continuation, such as "Tell me about ..."
   - Verifying beliefs, such as "You seem to believe ..."
   - Asking questions that systematically explore the transactions with the client such as:

       What did you do?
       What did the child do?
       How did the child respond?
       How did you respond?
       How did you feel?
       What did you do about the child's response?
       What was the child's reaction to your response?

2. *Techniques that elicit affect and encourage feeling.* These facilitate the consultee becoming aware of personal feelings and enable the consultant to express understanding, feelings, and empathy. Eliciting affect gets the whole person involved in the consultation.

   - Restatement of feeling
   - Reflection of feeling
   - Silence

3. *Techniques designed to facilitate self-understanding and awareness of one's own part in the transactions:*

   - Clarification, such as "You believe ..."
   - Restatement of content
   - Restatement of content and its hidden message
   - Questions that enable the consultee to see the psychological movement in transactions with the client

4. *Techniques designed to facilitate new responses.* Procedures for improving the consultee–client relationship and methods of modifying behavior:

   - Encouragement
   - Development of choices
   - Enlargement of consultee's view and presentation of alternatives
   - Establish goals
   - Establish procedures
   - Formulate change strategies

These leads must be accomplished with appropriate timing and sensitivity to the consultee. Techniques must account for the consultee's personality and willingness to change.

Leads are a function of the personality and theoretical bias of the consultant. They cannot be used mechanically. For example, development of choices is only effective when used in a climate where threat and fear are minimized and the relationship is not perceived to be judgmental. The evaluation and diagnosis are always done collaboratively. The consultant cannot prescribe for the consultee. Prescriptions or diagnosis without feedback and acceptance are ineffective.

CONSULTATION PROCESSES

In contrast to ineffective consultant/consultee communication patterns, goals are mutually aligned. The consultee participates in terms of perceptions, beliefs, values, and attitudes, which influence assumptions about students and the education process. When the consultee begins, the consultant listens closely. These opening statements influence the relationship. The probability of a collaborative diagnosis and treatment is being established. Early transactions are crucial. They must create a climate, establish communication, and set a pattern for ensuing contacts. At the same time, early transactions provide some help to the consultee with the current concern.

Consultants become highly directive, developing ready answers or instant solutions. "Give her more love," "Individualize the instruction," "Reinforce his good behavior" are quick replies. None of these "solutions" are necessarily bad, but they must be designed to fit the assets and liabilities involved in the transactions between consultant and consultee. Advice-driven answers may cause the consultee to consider the consultant's ideas as superficial.

The more active leads, such as disclosure, confrontation, and tentative hypotheses, may provoke resistance. When the consultant is involved in sharing perceptions, which come from an external frame of reference, these perceptions may be perceived as judgments or authoritarian statements. Resistance against a collaborative relationship may be the result. Active leads do not necessarily inhibit the consultation process if they are aligned with the consultee's personal meaning and subjective perceptions.

Confrontation can serve as a vehicle to bring the client in direct touch with personal experience. Honest confrontation can elicit constructive therapeutic process, movement, and ultimately constructive gain or change. These power factors in consultation may elicit dissonance. But confrontation can help the consultee become aware of the lack of harmony among goals, philosophy, and actions or practices.

The diagnosis is facilitated by the collaborative exploration of the current life situation, the perceptions of both client and consultee, and the open and honest feedback about any and all impressions that are generated. This phase is unique in its emphasis on searching for assets and strengths in the consultee and the client. The consultant must recognize that while the less active leads have less potential for harm, they also have greater potential for being circular, impotent, and unable to move the consultee toward awareness and new procedures.

FEELINGS OF ADEQUACY AND FAILURE

An increasing number of children and adolescents do not succeed in the educational process as it is presently organized. The evidence is apparent when one looks at problems related to underachievement, drug and alcohol abuse, dropouts, and the apathy of some students who remain within the system. Our society is regularly producing a large number of children and adults who perceive themselves as inadequate and failures.

William Glasser, a psychiatrist interested in education, drew some generalizations related to failure and discovered the following principle:

> Regardless of how many failures a person has had in his past, regardless of his background, his culture, his color, or his economic level, he will not succeed in general until he can in some way first experience success in one important part of his life. (1969, p. 5)

Glasser's contention was that if the child is able to succeed in school, that child will have an excellent chance for success in life. In contrast, failure in school diminishes the chance to be a success in life. Glasser (2000, 2005) continues to advocate his principles in his more recent publications.

The schools are a product of a failure-oriented evaluation system and a mistake-centered approach to instruction. Schools are more concerned with children's weaknesses and liabilities than with their strengths and assets. However, if schools are truly to meet the problems of the "rebel," the "unmotivated," the "apathetic," the "alienated," and the general social disorganization that surrounds us, they must start to examine the deficiencies that appear in parts of the educational system.

Our current emphasis on standards, threats, and punishment prevents the development of a feeling of genuine self-worth. Schools have failed to teach children how to maintain a successful identity and become socially responsible, contributing persons. Most children come to school feeling capable and comparatively adequate, but the school quickly creates feelings of inadequacy.

Schools can create persons who are truly committed to the learning process instead of memorization (Dinkmeyer & Carlson, 1990). In contrast, schools focus on memorization and failure and very seldom on problem solving, spontaneity, creativity, involvement, interest, and the capacity to think. In our overemphasis upon a mistake-centered type of education, which places emphasis upon the one right answer, we have failed to develop citizens who care, are concerned, and who are committed to action. An educated citizen in a democracy learns how to become an effective human being by participating in decision-making processes related to his or her own education. We learn how to decide by being given choices. We become responsible by accepting responsibility for the consequences of decisions, attitudes, and behavior.

STAGES OF THE CONSULTATION PROCESS

The consultation process can be broken into stages. General agreement does not exist as to what these stages are. Brown, Kurpius, and Morris (1988) suggested five or six steps, but also pointed out several established models that ignore some of these steps. For example, many consultation models stress the importance of building a relationship, while others ignore it.

Consider a basic, three-step process:

1. Initiate the relationship.
2. Respond to the problem or concern.
3. Analyze the results of your response.

This basic cycle is a useful point to begin the analysis of consultation styles and stages.

Several common characteristics of the process can be identified. First, the process can be seen as one of problem solving. Second, any definition of stages or steps must not use them as independent, discreet stages. The consultation may return to an earlier stage or jump ahead to a later stage. Finally, parallel processes between the consultant and consultee and the consultee and client must be recognized. Both relationships have stages.

Stages are neither arbitrary nor absolute. They reflect our understanding of the consultation process. Five stages are discussed: (1) establish the relationship, (2) gather data and identify the problem, (3) set goals, (4) use strategies, and (5) evaluation. The first stage is discussed in this chapter, with subsequent chapters dealing with the remaining stages.

ESTABLISH THE RELATIONSHIP

Most previous literature on consultation stresses the importance of establishing the relationship. Few have addressed the complex nature of the school consultant's role. This role may depend on whether the consultant is based within the building in which the consultation occurs.

If the consultant is not based in the particular school, one is perceived as an outsider. Many schools consist of 20 or more adult faculty and staff. They can become a tight-knit social system with norms and expectations. The norm "How do we feel about outside advice?" is worth examining.

Detecting this attitude may occur while developing the relationship. If the consultee has directly requested the consultation, the consultant is more likely to be accepted, at least initially. Acceptance may even be a topic for discussion while establishing the relationship.

Skills in this stage of the relationship can be drawn from previous counselor training. *Listening* and *attending* are important. Body language, eye contact, and reflective listening are all part of the consultant's abilities at this stage.

ETHICAL CONSIDERATION

The beginning of the relationship poses specific concerns for the consultant. *Confidentiality* is essential but often overlooked. The ground rules must be established so that both parties understand the limits. This issue is inherent in consultation; a third party is involved (Brown, 1993). The consultant must be careful to not promise total confidentiality. There are differences in ethical concerns between traditional counseling and consultation. The issue should be resolved in a process of mutual agreement. Confidentiality is essential, yet complex. A full discussion of this issue is found in Brown et al. (1988) and McCarthy and Sorenson (1993). We also urge full knowledge of your state laws concerning counselor–client confidentiality.

An example of the complexity of this issue follows. A teacher involves the counselor as a consultant regarding a child in the classroom. During the process of gathering data the consultant believes that the child's school problems may be in part due to abuse and neglect in the home. The consultant (or any adult) is bound by state law and school district policy to report any suspected child abuse. However, the teacher does not believe abuse is occurring and terminates the consultation relationship.

This example highlights the real risks and challenges in the consultation relationship. Whether an external or internal consultant, establishing the relationship includes a mutually agreed boundary for confidentiality.

Another issue to clarify at the beginning of a consultation relationship is *equality.* Consultation relationships strive for equality between the participants. Consultees often do not perceive their role as equal; they have a problem and are seeking answers. They see their part in the relationship as inferior.

This perceived less-than position makes the consultant's encouragement skills essential. Consultants can stress equality by directly stating this belief, or can imply the same through a variety of behaviors. Equality behaviors focus on recognizing assets and efforts, responsibility for the consultee, and encouragement through listening, structuring, and decision-making collaboration.

The third area of concern at the start of a consultation relationship concerns the *crossover* between counseling and consultation. It is recommended that consultants do not become counselors within the same relationship. This creates a dual relationship.

It is a difficult rule to follow, especially when one is trained as a counselor. The consultation relationship must focus on the third party, not the consultee. In theory, consultation and counseling are mutually exclusive (Newman, 1993).

What if a consultee presents a personal situation that leads itself to counseling? The consultant must realize the dangers on crossing over the line into counseling.

A consultant was asked to work with a seventh-grade teacher, Mrs. M. She presented challenges with two students and stated, "They make me so mad. They remind me of my kids." Here the consultant could take the focus off the two students and place it on Mrs. M's children, turning the relationship into counseling. The consultation would shift and the focus would be lost.

The consultant should use listening skills to establish credibility with the consultee. Should that listening include issues related to the consultee's personal life, it is not consultation. The consultant must either reframe the relationship, make a referral, or terminate the relationship.

The fourth concern at the beginning of consultation relationships is the necessity for *communication skills* by the consultant. Various texts do justice to this core counselor competency. To outline the necessary communication skills is not within the scope of this book. However, consultation cannot occur without communications competency.

Another issue relates to *cultural differences*. Differences between cultures exist and affect a consultant's ability to work effectively within the consultee's culture. Two examples from the authors demonstrate this situation:

- I was asked to consult with parents in a school district composed primarily of Hispanics in the United States southwest. Some of my information portrayed fathers playing an active role in home chores. This, I was told, was not the role fathers play in many of these families.
- Presenting similar materials in the Japanese culture presented challenges in the area of adolescent and child responsibilities. While a general agreement prevailed that children should have responsibility, little interest was expressed in allowing a child to experience consequences of choices, such as not doing homework. Parents said, "The stakes are too high. They can think for themselves once they have a good job."

Both incidents illustrate the consultant's cultural beliefs, contrasting with differing consultee cultural beliefs. This contrast raises an interesting question as to which view is "right."

Specific African American and white cultural concerns were raised by Gibbs (1980). The differences focus on the initial orientations to consultation. According to Gibbs, African Americans prejudge interpersonal competency and whites prejudge technical competency before committing to a consultation relationship. No proof of this theory is presented, but it highlights differences to which consultants must be sensitive. Although we are becoming more homogenized, be aware of differences that relate to culture.

Establishing the consultation relationship includes basic communication skills, confidentiality issues, and sensitivity to cultural issues. It also delineates the differences between consultation and counseling and maintains a finer difference between the two types of relationships.

SUMMARY

The consultant's role has been heavily researched and delineated throughout the literature for more than 20 years. We have highlighted major issues, including the nature of the relationship, its effectiveness, and steps in the consultation process. In the remainder of this book, we set forth our theory and practice of consultation.

REVIEW QUESTIONS

1. How are school counselors perceived by other school professionals?
2. What are the differences between elementary and high school counselors? How do you account for these differences, and what do they imply for a consultation relationship?
3. What do teachers see as desirable characteristics from consultants?
4. What are ineffective communication styles from consultants? Give examples whenever possible.
5. What are effective communication styles from consultants? Again, give examples.
6. Discuss both the unique and common characteristics of the stages of the consultation process.

REFERENCES

Bloom, B. (1977). Affective outcomes of school learning. *Phi Delta Kappan, 59,* 193–198.

Brown, D. (1993). Training consultants: A call to action. *Journal of Counseling and Development, 72,* 139–143.

Brown, D., Kurpius, D. J., & Morris, J. R. (1988). *Handbook of consultation with individuals and small groups.* Alexandria, VA: Association for Counselor Education and Supervision.

California Department of Education. (1990). *Toward a state of esteem: The final report of the Task force to promote self-esteem and personal and social responsibility.* Sacramento: Author.

Clemes, H., & Bean, R. (1981). *Self-esteem, the key to your child's well-being.* New York: Putnam.

Combs, A., & Soper, D. (1963). *The relationship of child perceptions to adjustment and behavior in early school years.* Washington, DC: Cooperative Research Project, Office of Health, Education and Welfare.

Dinkmeyer, D., Jr. (1987). *Consultation competency preferences from school teachers.* Unpublished manuscript.

Dinkmeyer, D., Jr., & Carlson, J. C. (1990). Guidance in a small school. *School Counselor, 37,* 199–203.

Dinkmeyer, D., & Dinkmeyer, D., Jr. (1982a). *Developing an understanding of self and others: DUSO 1.* Circle Pines, MN: American Guidance Service.

Dinkmeyer, D., & Dinkmeyer, D., Jr. (1982b). *Developing an understanding of self and others: DUSO 2.* Circle Pines, MN: American Guidance Service.

Gibbs, J. T. (1980). The interpersonal orientation in mental health consultation: Toward a model of ethnic variations in consultation. *Journal of Community Psychology, 8,* 195–207.

Glasser, W. (1969). *Schools without failure.* New York: Harper & Row.

Glasser, W. (2000). *Creating the competency based classroom.* Chatsworth, CA: William Glasser Institute.

Glasser, W. (2005). *Treating mental health as a public health problem: A new leadership role for the helping professions.* Chatsworth, CA: William Glasser Institute.

Hawes, D. (1989). Communication between teachers and children: A counselor consultant/ trainer model. *Elementary School Counseling and Guidance, 24,* 58–67.

Humphrey, N., Charlton, J., & Newton, I. (2004). The developmental roots of disaffection? *Educational Psychology, 24*(5), 579–595.

King, K. A. (1994). Self-concept and self-esteem: A clarification of terms. *Journal of School Health, 67*(2) 212–215.

McCarthy, M., & Sorenson, G. (1993). School counselors and consultants: Legal duties and liabilities. *Journal of Counseling and Development, 72,* 159–167.

Moeller, T. (1994). What research says about self-esteem and academic performance. *Education Digest, 59*(5), 34–38.

Newman, J. L. (1993). Ethical issues in consultation. *Journal of Counseling and Development, 72,* 148–196.

Satir, V. (1988). *The new peoplemaking.* New York: Science and Behavior Books.

Wiggins, J. (1987). Self-esteem, earned grades, and television viewing habits of students. *School Counselor, 35,* 129–133.

Wiggins, J., & Schatz, E. (1994). The relationship of self-esteem to grades, achievement scores, and other factors critical to school success. *School Counselor, 41*(4), 239–245.

3

A CONSULTATION THEORY

In this chapter, you will learn:

- ineffective consultant beliefs
- a rationale for the Adlerian approach
- effective consultant beliefs
- nine rules of behavior, including goals of misbehavior
- discipline strategies

Every consultant has a personal understanding of human behavior. This understanding is, in fact, a theory of human behavior. Your theory is based in part on life experiences, reading books, coursework in graduate school, and in-service workshops. If we add to these previous experiences a systematic, accurate set of beliefs, we have a concrete foundation for changing behaviors.

Theory for theory's sake has value only to the intellectual. *The consultant requires a theory that is practical.* This comprehensive yet practical understanding of human behavior is frequently lacking in consultation. Both consultant and teacher can be searching for a theory. Teachers, in their efforts to eliminate undesirable behaviors, may adapt a set of rules or regulations that appear to solve the problem. Pat answers, advice, and "quick-fix" solutions have no underlying understanding of behavior, misbehavior, and motivation. Today's solution does not necessarily solve tomorrow's challenge.

In this chapter, we present a practical theory of consultation based on what is referred to as Individual Psychology. Founded by Alfred Adler and developed across North America by Rudolf Dreikurs and others, Individual Psychology is well suited to the needs of the consultant. It offers theory on misbehavior, discipline, motivation, and relationships. The theory has concrete strategies or tactics for each of the consultation dimensions.

INEFFECTIVE BELIEFS

Many common beliefs about the cause of human behavior and misbehavior are ineffective. The "external frame of reference" is an example of such an approach. It is illustrated in the following example.

A student has high test scores but does not do well in school. This is contradictory information — the test scores show ability, yet the student is not performing. What is the explanation? The external frame of reference looks to causes outside the student for explanation. These causes might be a poor environment or home situation, poor relationships with peers or teachers, or any other reasons outside the student.

Externally based explanations for behavior and misbehavior include the following:

1. *Sex-role stereotype.* Although less prevalent today, teachers and parents may excuse male assertive misbehavior and female inadequacy behaviors simply because of gender. The phrase "boys will be boys" expresses such a lack of understanding. Stereotyping by gender can include athletic or intellectual ability or inability. It also encompasses behavior expectations: boys are uncooperative, girls are compliant.

2. *Heredity.* Our present understanding of genetics does not allow us to conclude it is a primary cause of behavior and misbehavior. Research in this area suggests tendencies and patterns, but it is not sufficient as a complete explanation for personality. It certainly does not give us directives for consultation.

3. *Environment.* Where the student lives, the socioeconomic status, two parents or one are not primary causes of behavior and misbehavior.

4. *Ages and stages.* Behavior is due to a particular age, such as the "terrible twos" or the challenging teenage years.

5. *Family failure.* Divorce, remarriage, two parents working, or single parent working all contribute to the belief the child is being harmed in this family of origin.

There are increasingly turbulent and negative external factors surrounding today's students. In the final analysis, however, these external factors are usually not the sole or predominant cause of a student's personality. Consultants have few, if any, effective recommendations or strategies if these external factors are the sole cause of the problem. If we believe the cause of the consultation issue is "because" of age, gender, or environment, what can be done? These are immovable variables. They explain away the problem and offer no viable solution.

The external frame of reference also looks for many facts and opinions. Case studies or staffings bring together many points of view. The emphasis is on opinions, preferably representing a nonbiased scientific approach.

For example, when a case study or an individual analysis is conducted, specialists from various disciplines (e.g., social work, administration, school psychologist) bring in facts and details as to how the student performs. Each brings a piece of the puzzling student. These pieces of the puzzle do not necessarily result in a coherent picture. The points made by each profession do not necessarily result in an accurate picture of the child's personality or decisions. Each may be "true," as seen by that adult, but the collective opinion may not present the child in the most helpful perspective.

Behavior is better understood through the internal frame of reference. How does the behavior "make sense" to that student? Because behavior is a function of an individual's perceptions, we seek to understand the student's and consultee's perceptions. Careful observation can identify the feelings, attitudes, and purposes of the student. Understanding behavior is a cornerstone of this approach.

RATIONALE FOR THE INDIVIDUAL PSYCHOLOGY APPROACH TO CONSULTATION

The purpose of the consultation process is to increase the human potential of the teacher, administrator, student, and parent. It also seeks to reduce stressors. Each individual has a considerable creative capacity to understand, to change, and to learn. When we begin a consultation relationship, we tap this creative capacity in the consultee. In turn, the skills we teach the consultee have an impact on those the consultee influences.

For example, Miss Warren may start a consultation relationship with a school counselor. She might want to change the behavior of several students in her classroom, believing the students are not functioning at their potential. The teacher is seeking change and comes to the consultant for that change. Thus we find the basis for a beginning in the consultation relationship, a desire for change.

The recognition that a "problem" exists is a basis for the relationship between consultant and consultee. In Chapter 1 we identified three parts to the consulting relationship: consultant, consultee, and "problem/person." Effective consulting relationships separate the problem from the person.

For example, a teacher comes to the consultant with a "problem student." Is the consultation problem:

1. the student,
2. the student's beliefs that fuel the undesirable behaviors,
3. the teacher's beliefs about the student and student's behaviors, or
4. the teacher's lack of effective behaviors to deal with the student?

The four possibilities may confuse the basic "problem" in the consultation.

In the Adlerian approach, *beliefs* are examined in addition to behaviors. We collect data on behaviors that reveal the inherent beliefs. In this case of the "problem student," descriptions of behaviors give a better picture of the teacher and student beliefs as to what generates these behaviors.

EFFECTIVE CONSULTANT BELIEFS

Your behavior is influenced by your belief system. Effective consultants have different beliefs about people than ineffective consultants. For example, are all people capable? Refusal to allow others to function (by taking on all the responsibility yourself) would be inconsistent with that belief. Another example is recommending better listening skills, but exhibiting poor listening skills in a conversation with the teacher:

Teacher: They sure make me angry!

Consultant: I suggest you give them more love.

Teacher: I'll try! But they really make me angry.

Consultant: It's also important to listen and hear their feelings.

Teacher: Yes, but they still make me mad!

The consultant failed to hear the teacher's feeling or to realize that the proposed suggestion was not congruent with the teacher's problem. The consultant believed it was important to listen and hear feelings, but did not hear the anger in the teacher's statement.

A more effective dialogue would include the consultant hearing the immediate feelings of the teacher:

Teacher: They sure make me angry!

Consultant: You're angry about your students.

Teacher: Yes, they just don't listen. Some seem to want to make me mad.

The consultant deals directly with the teacher's anger. It leads to clues as to what beliefs the students have when angering the teacher.

An effective approach also allows for erroneous judgments and has the ability to modify a faulty tentative hypothesis. Here the consultant misjudges the intensity of the teacher's feelings:

Teacher: They make me angry!

Consultant: You're absolutely furious at your students.

Teacher: No, I don't let them get to me. I'd be crazy by now.

Consultant: But there are times when they do things that make you angry.

Teacher: Yes.

The consultant misjudged the intensity of feelings. Rather than convince the teacher that the assessment was correct, the consultant corrects and tries again. The consultee confirms the second effort.

Even if the teacher does get angry at the students (the consultant may know this from the principal, parents, or other observers), it is more helpful to begin with the consultee's own perceptions. In consultation, do we focus on the student, the teacher, or both? In counseling, the counselor helps people to understand themselves and to modify their behaviors. In consulting, the consultant helps the consultee to directly understand self, others, the relationship between self and others, and procedures to modify behavior.

A practical consultation theory includes:

- an understanding of human behavior
- a procedure that helps the consultant to accurately communicate this understanding to others
- operational knowledge of how to implement or put this understanding into practice

UNDERSTANDING HUMAN BEHAVIOR

Begin with this assertion: *Nobody ever throws away a behavior that works.*

The following ideas elaborate on this part of the Adlerian theory of behavior:

1. Human personality is understood by its unity or pattern — the lifestyle.
2. Behavior is goal-directed and purposeful.
3. The individual is constantly striving for significance.
4. All behavior has social meaning.
5. We always have a choice.
6. Belonging is a basic need.
7. Understanding behavior is based on idiographic, not nomothetic laws.
8. Look at use, not potential.
9. Social interest is the indicator of mental health.

Notice how the beliefs of the consultant and the consultee are critical to understanding and changing behaviors. In our experience, many of these ideas, explored in some detail below, have never been known to consultees. Therefore, the consultation relationship has a strong educational emphasis.

1. Human Personality Is Understood by Its Unity or Pattern — The Lifestyle

Instead of analyzing elements of a person's personality, look at the *pattern*. Historically, school personnel have looked at the student as a collection of pieces — test scores, IQ scores, past grades, and teacher comments. When these are viewed individually, they have little meaning. Effective consultants look for the pattern to the pieces. This pattern is the personality. An early elementary school student has a definable personality. We believe that personality is defined by the time a child is five or six years old. Therefore, virtually every student in the school presents a fixed, measurable character. This definable personality is the lifestyle. An individual's lifestyle also can be seen as a characteristic pattern of beliefs and choices. For example, "I am a troublemaker" or "I can help people" are beliefs that contribute to a lifestyle.

If your prior training is not in counseling, you may have been exposed to different theories and ideas about personality development (although counseling itself has many ideas about personality, too). For example, the nurse approaches the individual from a physiological standpoint, the social worker from a social relationship approach, and the psychologist from a psychological standpoint. Each profession understands a piece of the puzzle.

A person is more than health, social relationships, or mental abilities. The total being has thoughts, feelings, and beliefs working in concert to maintain the lifestyle. We must understand the pattern and help the person in relation to this pattern or lifestyle.

The unity or pattern of a student's behavior is therefore often misunderstood. Equally important, the consultant can misunderstand the pattern of a consultee's behaviors if the broadest possible picture is not examined. The story of the blind men at the elephant illustrates this point. To one man, elephants were thick and stout (feeling only the leg); to another, long and thin (discovering just the tail), and to another very sharp (encountering the tusk). The pieces were very different and contradictory. Considered together, however, they give a truer picture of the elephant.

Labels and categories for students contribute to a fragmentary analysis of behaviors. Students can be considered "underachievers," "scholars," or other common descriptors. How could a scholar get in trouble after school, and how could an underachiever do so well on that test (he or she must have been cheating)? A piece of the puzzle creates misleading and useless conclusions. The unity and pattern of any person, including young students, is expressed through the lifestyle.

2. Behavior Is Goal-Directed and Purposeful

The Adlerian approach stresses the purposive (goal-directed) nature of behavior. This goal may not be known to the behaver, but it does not prevent the person from seeking the goal. The goal-directedness of behavior applies to misbehavior as well as positive behavior.

Goal-directedness is an essential, important concept for the consultant. It offers new perceptions on seemingly confusing behaviors. In many ways, goals of behavior are both an assessment and an answer to many consultees' questions. Goals are clues to a person's intention (the assessment) and what can be done about it (the answer).

Consultation with teachers and parents often concerns misbehaviors. Understanding the misbehavior purposefully helps both the consultant and consultee. It also allows the consultee to understand how corrective actions might be taken.

Bruce has become a problem for his teacher. He does not do his homework and is frequently argumentative in the classroom. When the teacher asks Bruce why he hasn't done his homework, he replies, "I don't want to do it, and you can't make me." The teacher replies, "You can't say that to me. If you don't do your homework, I'm going to call your parents." As the teacher walks away, Bruce has a sly smile on his face.

The purpose of Bruce's misbehavior is power. He is engaged in a power struggle with his teacher, demonstrating who is in control. When the teacher brings more power into the conflict (by threatening to contact the parents), Bruce is pleased at this powerful response. Whether his parents are concerned with his schoolwork, or not, he has created a power struggle. This attempt by the teacher to defeat his powerful resistance will not work.

In most consultations, the goals of misbehavior are an essential part of the diagnostic relationship. Goal-directed behavior helps the consultant to understand the third party. It gives a frame of reference for both consultant and consultee to work with the problem.

Two final concepts are addressed in the context of behavior. Every individual behaves according to his or her own private logic; the unwritten set of rules that constitute the lifestyle. The creative capacity to choose is also at work in lifestyle development.

The Four Goals of Misbehavior   Rudolf Dreikurs found that misbehavior in children occurs to achieve one of four goals: *attention, power, revenge,* or *to display inadequacy.* When asked how he determined the goals, Dreikurs said, "I did not invent them, I merely observed them."

Dreikurs and others within Individual Psychology have discussed goals of misbehavior in numerous articles, books, and workshops. One of these discussions is in Dinkmeyer, McKay, and Dinkmeyer's *The Parent's Handbook* (1998). Although that context is parent and child, the student/teacher and consultant/consultee relationships are applicable. The concept and others related to teaching are most thoroughly discussed in Dinkmeyer et al. (1998).

Because all people are social, decision-making beings, our decisions about behavior are based on our views on how to belong, to find a place of significance. If this belonging can be done positively, fine. If belonging is achieved through negative behavior (in the behaver's perception), fine, too. Misbehavior comes from a perception, or belief, of discouragement.

We can look at misbehavior from three perspectives: the belief behind the behavior, the behavior itself, or the payoff (goal or consequence) of the behavior. The most helpful procedure is to first look at the goal or consequence of the behavior.

In Table 3.1, The Goals of Misbehavior, the essential elements of misbehavior — the child's goals and faulty beliefs and the parents' feelings and alternatives — are outlined. To identify a specific goal, use this two-step method:

TABLE 3.1 The Goals of Misbehavior

Child's Faulty Goal	Child's Goal	Parent's Feelings and Reaction	Child's Response to Parent's Attempts at Correction	Alternative for Parents
I belong *only* when I am being noticed or served.	Attention	Feeling: annoyed. Reaction: tendency to remind and coax.	Temporarily stops misbehavior or disturbs in another way.	Ignore misbehavior when possible. Give attention for positive behavior when child is not making a bid for it. Avoid undue service. Realize that reminding, punishing, rewarding, coaxing, and service are undue attention.
I belong *only* when I am in control or am boss, or when I am proving no one can boss me!	Power	Feeling: angry, provoked, as if one's authority is threatened. Reaction: tendency to fight or give in.	Active- or passive-aggressive misbehavior is intensified, or child submits with "defiant compliance."	Withdraw from conflict. Help child see how to use power constructively by appealing for child's help and enlisting cooperation. Realize that fighting or giving in only increases child's desire for power.
I belong *only* by hurting others as I feel hurt. I cannot be loved.	Revenge	Feeling: deeply hurt. Reaction: tendency to retaliate and get even.	Seeks further revenge by intensifying misbehavior or choosing another weapon.	Avoid feeling hurt. Avoid punishment and retribution. Build trusting relationship; convince child that he or she is loved.
I belong *only* by convincing others not to expect anything from me; I am helpless.	Display of inadequacy	Feeling: despair, hopelessness; "I give up." Reaction: tendency to agree with child that nothing can be done.	Passively responds or fails to respond to whatever is done. Shows no improvement.	Stop all criticism. Encourage any positive attempt, no matter how small; focus on assets. Above all, don't be hooked into pity and don't give up.

Source: Don Dinkmeyer and Gary D. McKay, *Systematic Training for Effective Parenting (STEP): The Parent's Handbook,* American Guidance Service, Inc., © 1998. Reproduced with permission. All rights reserved.

- What is your reaction to the child's misbehavior? What do you feel, and do, when the child misbehaves?
- What does the child do in response to your behaviors?

In Table 3.1, the four goals are described in terms of feelings and reactions. Goals appear to increase in intensity from attention to power and revenge, whereas the fourth goal seems less intense. Annoyed is a less intense feeling than anger. Hopelessness seems less than anger, though. This progression is increasing discouragement about belonging in the classroom or other group in a positive way.

3. The Individual Is Constantly Striving for Significance

Individuals strive for success. This movement is part of an individual's perceived (objectively or subjectively) feeling of being less than others and a need to become more than those around oneself.

Significance has its roots in our early and formative years. We are born a helpless individual, truly dependent upon the caring and attention of others to survive. In many ways, it is an accurate perception that one is "less than" others. As we grow, we seek to become equal to those around us, while seeking a unique place in that group.

In contrast to theories that emphasize the "push" of events from the past, Adlerian psychology recognizes the "pull" of the future. The significance of behavior lies in terms of the consequences or how the student is seeking to be known. The concern is less with the actual behavior and more with emphasis on the direction in which the individual is moving. This movement is the striving for significance (Dinkmeyer & Sperry, 2000).

Consultants and consultees benefit from a concrete visualization of this process. For example, the consultant can ask the consultee to imagine the student wearing a T-shirt. If the T-shirt's message was the student's belief, what might it say? "I want attention" or "I want to give up" are some of the messages students wear.

To create a "flip-side" to these beliefs, the imagined T-shirt can be turned inside out. Here we find the alternatives for the teacher. "I want attention" becomes "Catch me being good," and "I want to give up" becomes "I need lots of encouragement."

Expectations are powerful influences on the misbehaver. When one works with "where the person is headed" (the goal), the involvement is deeper and more significant than attempting to only deal with present behaviors. The consultant is working with "where you will be going, and what you will be doing," in addition to "what you are feeling right now." The striving for significance becomes a motivating force.

While we all do not seek to be significant in the same way, we do seek to establish a sense of importance. The striving for significance is consistent with the seven goals of teen misbehavior (see Table 3.2). The student is looking for a place in the classroom. Therefore, the consultant asks the question, "How is the child seeking to become significant, or known, in this classroom?"

4. All Behavior Has Social Meaning

Students act in a social context. Behaviors are for the "benefit" of peers and adults. If a student seeks to attract attention, others must pay attention if the goal is to succeed. Behavior does not operate in a vacuum. It is intended to have an impact on others. The "behavior is never thrown away if it works" idea reinforces this concept.

Behavior is influenced by the consequences and reactions of other people. The social meaning of behavior can be discovered in the interactions between the teacher and student, and the student and peers. Students seek to belong to each other. Groups, clubs, teams, friendships all illustrate this basic human need. At the same time, each individual will strive to be unique; this is sometimes called "striving from a felt minus to a perceived plus." This is a particularly powerful influence as adolescents move through a process called *individuation*. It can go to extremes, at all times reflecting the individual's decisions to become unique. Tattoo this concept in your mind.

5. We Always Have a Choice

The student creatively interacts with the environment. Behavior is not only reactive or responsive to an external stimulus. Each individual has the capacity to creatively respond. Behavior is never understood solely within the framework of stimulus-response (S-R). It is understood in terms of a stimulus-organism-response (S-O-R). The person (organism) is exercising a choice or decision.

Teachers and parents may not, at first, understand this idea. If the adult does not understand a child's goal or purpose, it is maintained or reinforced by the adult's behavior. This can increase the teacher's or parent's frustration. Misbehavior can grow stronger rather than weaker. The objective response to misbehavior is part of the solution. The unique meaning and significance that each individual derives from the misbehavior is also part of the solution.

Many consultees come to the relationship seeing absolutely no choices in their current situation. They are stuck in a pattern that is not changing or improving.

TABLE 3.2 The Goals of Teen Misbehavior

		The Basic Four Goals		
Teen's Faulty Goal	Goal	Example	Parent's Feelings and Reactions	Teens Response to Parent's Reactions
I belong only when: I am being noticed or served.	Attention	Attention: clowning, minor mischief, unique dress. Passive: forgetting, neglecting chores.	Annoyed.	Temporarily stops behavior. Later repeats behavior or does something else to attract attention.
I am in control or proving no one can control me.	Power	Active: aggressive defiance, disobedience, hostility. Passive: stubbornness, resistance.	Angry, provoked. Fight power with power or give in.	If parent fights, teen intensifies or submits with "defiant compliance." If parent gives in, teen stops.
I hurt others as I feel hurt. I don't feel loved or lovable.	Revenge	Active: hurtfulness, rudeness, violence, destructiveness. Passive: staring hurtfully at others.	Deeply hurt.	Seeks further revenge by intensifying attack or choosing another weapon.
I convince others not to expect anything from me. I am unable and helpless.	Display of inadequacy	Passive only: quitting easily, avoiding trying. Being truant or dropping out of school. Escaping through drugs.	Despairing, hopeless, discouraged. Agree with teen that nothing can be done. Give up. (With drug abuse, may take teen for help.)	Continues passive, inadequate, and discouraged behaviors.

(Continued)

Additional Goals

Teen's Faulty Goal	Goal	Example	Parent's Feelings and Reactions	Teens Response to Parent's Reactions
I create widespread peer misbehavior.	Excitement	Avoiding routing. Showing interest in alcohol, other drugs, promiscuous sex, daredevil sports, exciting events, and activities.	Nervous, angry, hurt. What will happen next? Is on guard. May share excitement about positive endeavors.	Resists or continues exciting misbehavior. (May become power contest.)
I have widespread peer acceptance.	Peer Acceptance	Constantly attempting to obtain widespread peer acceptance.	Approval (if parent agrees with choice of friends). Worried, anxious (if disapproves of friends). Try to get teen to seek new friends.	Resists or continues to see friends. (May become power contest.)
I am the best at everything (or better than most).	Superiority	Striving for best grades, most honors. Putting down parents and others. Using superior talents against others.	Approval, inadequacy. Praise. Attempt to put teen in his place.	Continues striving. Continues putting down others to defend own self-image.

Adlerian consultants believe there is always a choice, even if not initially recognized. One way to access this is through perceptual alternatives.

One final example illustrates how we often miss choices. If a person is stuck in a dilemma, unsure about doing one thing or another, how many choices do they have? Many see two; consultants see three. The third position, "stuck on the horns of the dilemma," often makes it possible to remain passive or unresolved.

6. Belonging Is a Basic Need

A person's primary group is the family. The secondary group is often a daycare, nursery, school, or similar peer setting. The socialization process of daycare centers, prekindergartens, nursery schools, and elementary schools is the setting for each child's search to belong in the group. The process of finding a place in the classroom group is continuous. Classrooms change from year to year, even day to day. Students grow and exercise their rights as unique individuals. Adolescents have the challenge of finding a place with peer groups. Even the popular high school quarterback is faced with the process of finding another way to belong within the collegiate community, work setting, or another group to which he must gain a feeling of belonging. One never graduates from the need to belong within the group.

Belonging in the classroom can be illustrated in the four goals of misbehavior. What explains the class clown, the class bully, or other seemingly undesirable positions? Using private logic and subjective perception, the child decides upon his or her best chance at a unique place in the group. An unwritten rule that can explain seemingly poor behaviors is "It is better to be notorious than unnoticed!"

7. Understanding Behavior Is Based on Idiographic, Not Nomothetic Laws

In understanding human behavior, principles of an idiographic nature (principles that apply to the individual's unique lifestyle) are of more concern than those of a nomothetic nature (laws that apply generally). Normative group descriptions cannot be universally applied to the individual. While knowing about the average 10-year-old is interesting, that type of data cannot be translated immediately into corrective procedures and practice.

Nomothetic laws do not lend much help in understanding the behavior of the individual, from that individual's point of view. Commonly held beliefs such as "the terrible twos" or "all 9-year-olds ..." are less useful than beliefs based in observations of a specific 2- or 9-year-old's behaviors. Consultants look at both how the individual appears to self, and how that person appears to others.

8. Look at Use, Not Potential

Many students have been identified by the label "underachiever." The attributes a person possesses are less important than what that person decides to do with the endowment. We can only deal with what is, not what isn't. Ability cannot be equated with interest. If a child has "high potential" but the potential is not reflected in grades, what is accomplished by telling the child that he or she is not living up to potential?

An individual may choose to not live up to specific capacity for subjective reasons:

> Meliska was the third child from a family with musical interests and abilities. When she entered the fourth grade, her parents placed her in band. She soon was a disruptive force in band class; the teacher sent a note home saying, "Meliska has to learn to cooperate, or she will have to quit band." Her parents were mystified; Meliska had often imitated her older siblings and had been interested in band. However, they were able to learn that band was the same time as art, and she didn't want to miss art.

What the child does with ability is important. What that maximum potential ability might be is less important. The consultant looks at the use, not the potential.

9. Social Interest Is the Indicator of Mental Health

The development of social interest is crucial for the individual's mental health. Social interest can be defined as the ability to cooperate with others. As consultants, we demonstrate this ability in our consultation relationships. Teachers and parents can express confidence in the child's ability to develop social interest.

This ability can be encouraged by specific beliefs about students. Although presented as teacher beliefs about students, the following four ideas equally apply to other relationships:

- I believe students can make decisions.
- I am equal, not more or less than others.
- I believe in mutual respect.
- I am human. I have the "courage to be imperfect" (Dinkmeyer et al., 2000).

DISCIPLINE

Many consultees present problems that involve discipline situations. Discipline is an integral part of schools. Many surveys and public opinion polls rate it as the biggest challenge in our schools.

We believe discipline is an educational process. The consultant teaches the consultee an approach (or theory) to discipline. In turn, the consultee uses this approach with the third party. Often this means the school counselor teaches the teacher how to work with the students.

In recent years, a wide variety of systems have been offered to schools that focus on a specific set of rules for more effective discipline. This approach may not be as effective as the system we propose.

The discipline system we advocate uses *natural and logical consequences.* In contrast to punishment, consequences are an educational process that capitalizes on the student's inherent tendency to *choose* behaviors. With properly applied consequences, no choices are "bad." Each choice is a learning experience. The differences between punishment and consequences are expressed in Table 3.3.

NATURAL AND LOGICAL CONSEQUENCES

When consultees present discipline situations, natural and logical consequences usually apply. In this section, natural and logical consequences are defined and examples are presented.

Children learn and grow through the use of natural and logical consequences. Consequences represent the reality of the social order (logical consequences) or the natural course of events without outside interference (natural consequences).

What are natural consequences? Staying up late, you feel tired the next morning. Getting caught in a rainstorm without an umbrella, you get wet. Forgetting to eat, you feel hungry. These examples show the natural order of the world. No one has made you tired, wet, or hungry. It is just the way the world works.

What are logical consequences? Students who throw food must clean it up. If you fight at recess, you lose a recess (and have the chance to try again tomorrow). If you do not turn in a paper at an established deadline, you get a zero. These examples show the logical relationship between the deed and the discipline. No one has "made" the student throw food, fight, or forget. And the relationship between the behavior and the consequence is a logical one.

TABLE 3.3 Major Differences between Punishment and Logical Consequences

Punishment			Logical Consequences		
Characteristics	Underlying Message	Likely Results	Characteristics	Underlying Message	Likely Results
1. Emphasis on power or personal authority.	Do what I say because I say so! I'm in charge here!	Rebellion; revenge lack of self-discipline; sneakiness; irresponsibility.	1. Emphasis on reality of social order.	I trust you to learn to respect yourself and the rights of others.	Self-discipline; cooperation; respect for self and others; reliability.
2. Rarely related to the act; arbitrary.	I'll show you! You deserve what you're getting!	Resentment; revenge; fear; confusion; rebellion.	2. Logically related to misbehavior; makes sense.	I trust you to make responsible choices.	Learns from experience.
3. Implies moral judgments.	This should teach you! You're bad!	Feelings of hurt, resentment, guilt, revenge.	3. No moral judgment. Treats student with dignity.	You are a worthwhile person!	Learns behavior; may be objectionable (not to self).
4. Emphasizes past behavior.	This is for what you did — I'm not forgetting! You'll never learn!	Feels unable to make good decisions. Unacceptable in eyes of teacher.	4. Concerned with present and future behavior.	You can make your your own choices and take care of yourself.	Becomes self-directed and self-evaluating.

(Continued)

TABLE 3.3 Major Differences between Punishment and Logical Consequences (*Continued*)

Punishment			Logical Consequences		
Characteristics	Underlying Message	Likely Results	Characteristics	Underlying Message	Likely Results
5. Threatens disrespect, either open or implied.	You'd better shape up! No one in my class acts like that!	Desire to get even; fear; rebellion; guilt feelings.	5. Voice communicates respect and goodwill.	It's your behavior I don't like, but I still like you!	Feels secure in teacher's respect and support.
6. Demands compliance.	Your preferences don't matter! You can't be trusted to make wise decisions!	Defiant compliance; plans to get even another time; destruction of trust and equality.	6. Presents a choice.	You can decide.	Responsible decisions; increased resourcefulness.

Source: Don Dinkmeyer, Gary D. McKay, and Don Dinkmeyer, Jr., *Systematic Training for Effective Teaching (STET): Teacher's Handbook*. CMTI Press, Inc., © 2000. Reproduced with permission. All rights reserved.

Additional examples of logical consequences may be helpful. If the child writes on the wall, he or she must clean it up. Forgets gym shoes — play the game in socks. This is not another name for punishment. Dreikurs and Gray (1968) indicated five fundamental differences between logical consequences and punishment.

1. Logical consequences express the reality of the social order, not of the person. Punishment expresses the power of personal authority.
2. Logical consequences are logically related to the misbehavior, punishment rarely is.
3. Logical consequences imply no element of moral judgment; punishment often does.
4. Logical consequences are concerned only with what will happen now; punishment, with the past.
5. Consequences are invoked with a friendly voice; punishment with anger — either open or concealed.

In punishment, perhaps the child who forgets gym shoes would be asked to stay after school or write a paper about the importance of remembering. Logical consequences relate to the act. The child is motivated through the reality of life and not the mandate of an authority.

A good relationship between the teacher and child is an essential predecessor to a consequence-based discipline system. This relationship allows both students and teachers to understand and accept the consequences before they are applied. In a poor relationship, such as when a power conflict exists, the logical consequences turn into punishments, no matter how logical. Consequences must be applied consistently. The child must understand the logical consequences, and the teacher needs to be patient and allow time for the behavior to diminish. A misbehavior does not always disappear immediately.

COMPREHENSIVE DISCIPLINE IS EDUCATIONAL

A comprehensive approach to discipline is an educational process. The consultant must continue to offer the consultee opportunities to work with the consultant so that this education proceeds with an emphasis on *prevention*, not only remediation.

Students can be involved in the discipline process by a variety of methods that seek to involve their cooperation and collaboration. For example, a process as simple as asking students for their ideas on the order in which some materials are to be studied is a discipline method. This is an idea most consultees do not, initially, consider "discipline."

But it is part of a comprehensive approach that understands the theory behind effective discipline.

Some ideas that contribute to this discipline process include student involvement in issues such as:

- time spent on certain topics
- ways to study these topics
- the order of study
- methods of evaluation
- activities and projects
- committees and small groups
- classroom jobs
- seating arrangements

For example, one teacher reports she has had increased cooperation by allowing students to choose which examples in a workbook they will be doing. Instead of telling students "Do the first 10 problems on page 143," this teacher says "Do any 10 problems on page 143."

Comprehensive discipline is more than consequences or choices offered in a preventative mode. At the point of misbehavior, the teacher has several options. First, teachers and consultants should seek to understand the purpose, or goal, of the misbehavior. Goal diagnosis, discussed earlier in this chapter, is a vital clue in the teacher's response. In addition to the directives offered through goal diagnosis, four other approaches can be used:

1. *Reflective listening.* This will be presented in Chapter 5. It would be most appropriate for the goals of revenge or display of inadequacy.
2. *I-messages.* Also discussed in Chapter 5, the approach allows the teacher to communicate constructively with the student.
3. *Exploring alternatives.* This approach helps decide whether the problem at hand is a student problem, a shared problem (teacher and student), or a teacher problem.
4. Natural and logical consequences.

Effective discipline approaches are presented in Table 3.4.

SUMMARY

Consultants function from their own frame of reference. An understanding of an effective practical psychology can enhance this approach. The Adlerian approach offers such a theory for the consultant. Although simple, the approach allows the consultant to engage the

TABLE 3.4 Effective Approaches to Classroom Challenges

Approach	Purpose	Example
Reflective listening	Communicating understanding of students' feelings about the problems they face.	"You feel very sad because your friend says he doesn't like you anymore."
I-message	Communicating your feel-ings to students about how their behavior affects you.	(To the class) "When you are not interested in my lesson, I feel very discouraged because I've worked hard to prepare it."
Exploring alter-natives	Helping students decide how to solve a problem they own or negotiating agreements with students for teacher-owned problems.	"What are some ways you could solve your problem?" Or, "How could we settle our disagreement?"
Natural and logical consequences	Allowing students within limits to decide how they will behave and permit-ting them to experience the results of their decisions.	Natural: Students who fight may get hurt. Logical: Students who fight go to the talk-it-over area.
Giving permission to misbehave	Doing the unexpected by permitting misbehavior under certain conditions.	A student who swears is invited to go to a corner of the room to practice swearing.
Acknowledging the student's power	Admitting defeat or vulnerability in an effort to defuse the student's attempt to overpower, get revenge, or show superiority.	"You've proved your point. I can't force you to work."
Creating alterna-tives; turning a minus into a plus	Channeling misbehavior and mistaken goals in constructive directions.	The student who uses humor to disrupt can be put in charge of a comic classroom play.

Source: Don Dinkmeyer, Gary D. McKay, and Don Dinkmeyer, Jr., *Systematic Training for Effective Teaching (STET): Teacher's Handbook.* CMTI Press, Inc., © 2000. Reproduced with permission. All rights reserved.

consultee and understand the consultee in both simple and complex situations.

This theory is comprehensive. Solutions to problems come from the consultant's thorough knowledge of the theory. Individual Psychology has these elements, including the four goals of misbehavior, the concept of motivation through encouragement, and the holistic approach to the individual. The theory, including an approach to discipline, has been outlined in this chapter.

REVIEW QUESTIONS

1. What are two ineffective beliefs about behavior, and how would they hamper a consultation relationship?
2. Give two effective beliefs about human behavior.
3. What are the key differences between a consultation and counseling relationship?
4. Cite two of the nine ideas about behavior, and compare them with your prior ideas about behavior.
5. What is meant by a discipline "system"?
6. Besides natural and logical consequences, what other approaches to discipline can be used by the consultant?

REFERENCES

Dinkmeyer, D., & McKay, G. (1998). *Parenting teenagers*. Circle Pines, MN: American Guidance Service.

Dinkmeyer, D., & McKay, G. D. (1998). *Systematic training for effective parenting of teens (STEP/Teens): Parenting teenagers*. Circle Pines, MN: American Guidance Service.

Dinkmeyer, D., & McKay, G. D. (1998). *Systematic training for effective parenting (STEP): The parent's handbook*. Circle Pines, MN: American Guidance Service.

Dinkmeyer, D., McKay, G., & Dinkmeyer, D., Jr. (1998). *The parent's handbook*. Circle Pines, MN: American Guidance Service.

Dinkmeyer, D., McKay. G., & Dinkmeyer, D., Jr. (2000). *Systematic training for effective teaching (STET): Teacher's handbook*. Coral Springs, FL: CMTI Press.

Dinkmeyer, D., Jr., & Sperry, L. (2000). *Counseling and psychotherapy: An integrated individual psychology approach* (3rd ed.). Columbus, OH: Merrill.

Dreikurs, R., & Gray, L. (1968). *Psychology in the classroom*. New York: Harper & Row.

4

INDIVIDUAL CONSULTATION

In this chapter, you will learn:

- the nature of the helping relationship
- basic consultation procedures
- the seven-step consulting process
- three types of consultations
- the importance of lifestyle
- the nature of the helping relationship
- techniques for creating an effective relationship

BASIC PROCEDURES FOR INDIVIDUAL CONSULTING

The consultant must have a clear understanding of the consultation task. In the most basic terms, consultant A helps consultee B with challenge C. A and B collaborate so that C "gets better." C is often a student or parent. A, B, and C are all part of a "system." The system can be defined as the set of relationships between all persons in the school building. Each person interacts with others, demonstrating degrees of skill and success, failures and frustration. The consultant assesses the role and expectation of four major elements in the school system:

1. the principal
2. the teacher

3. the parents
4. the consultant (self) within this system

Teachers often focus on students, and parents often focus on teachers. Most often, consultees do not focus on themselves.

Consultants understand how to develop a collaborative relationship with the consultee. Cooperation and a commitment toward changing the system are part of the relationship. Working within the system, the consultant creates change with the consultees. This changes the system, with the cooperation of the consultee.

Consulting is similar, but different from counseling. It is also a helping relationship. Instead of focusing on self, consultees come to change a third party — the student. A and B do not focus on B, they focus on C.

IS IT COUNSELING OR CONSULTATION?

The relationship between the counselor and teacher (or parent, or administrator) can be confusing when specific premises are omitted. These simple rules help explain the differences between counseling and consultation.

It's consultation when:

- the main focus of the relationship is a third person (often a student);
- the relationship is characterized by collaboration on ways to help this third person.

In consultation, the counselor is a consultant and the other adult (teacher, parent, or administrator) is the consultee.

It's counseling when:

- the main focus of the relationship is the person seeking the help;
- the relationship is characterized by collaboration on ways to help the person seeking the help. While a third person may be discussed, the goal of the relationship is focused on the help seeker.

In counseling, the counselor is a counselor and the person seeking the help is the client. The terms "helper" or "consultant" can also be used to describe the counselor.

The collaborative relationship initiated by A is based upon A's beliefs about how to change behavior, attitudes, and beliefs. Consultation is effective when cooperative problem-solving approaches are used. It is impeded by advice-giving or superior-inferior methods. The teacher is not someone who needs to be "advised" but rather "consulted." A superficial string of answers or advice does not solve the consultee's concern. Teachers need more than ideas. Consultants help Bs integrate new ideas with their beliefs and emotions.

CONSULTATION TRAPS

The consultant does not "play expert." Some consultants who are always engaged in "crises" are often those whose lifestyles seek excitement or creating dependent relationships. Consultants must be aware of their beliefs and relationship style.

It can be flattering to receive a request for help with a problem. It can be gratifying to think that we might be able to provide a ready answer and solve the problem for the consultee. This is a trap the consultant must avoid. To avoid this and other traps, consultants must understand basic issues such as who is the client, who initiates the consultation, and basic strategies for effective consultation.

THE SEVEN-STEP CONSULTING PROCESS

Individual consultation with teachers (or parents) follows a seven-step process:

1. Establish the tone

   - Mutual respect — establish rapport or perceived equality.
   - Privacy and confidentiality are established.
   - Open, honest, and direct communication occurs.
   - This is an educational process and not a medical diagnosis.
   - Nobody will be blamed and everyone can be part of the solution.
   - Understand "How is this a problem for you (the teacher or parent)?"

2. Set a specific description of the problem.

   - Ask the consultee, "Can you give a specific example of when he or she was a problem for you? Pick something in the last day or two."
     a. Specifically/exactly, what did the student say or do?
     b. How did you feel when responding?
     c. What did he or she do then?

   - Say the exact words and say them in the way that you said them. (If the consultee can't remember, ask for a paraphrase.)

3. Get a second specific example

4. Clarify the goal of misbehavior and the teacher's (parent's) troubling belief.
5. Review the guidelines for reaching this goal:

  - Attention — catch them being good; create attention-getting moments.
  - Power — give them choices; create choice opportunities; don't fight or give in.
  - Revenge — give chances for fairness; refuse to be hurt.
  - Display of inadequacy — don't give up despite extreme discouragement; instead, ask, "One asset is …?"
  - Identify ways the consultee has successfully worked through this goal of misbehavior in other situations.
  - Review what could be done that the consultee has not yet done.

6. Solicit tentative suggestions.

  - Work on one problem at a time.
  - Break this into a realistic, one-week achievable step.
  - Be concrete.
  - Anticipate things getting worse before showing improvement.
  - Any changes are only for one week and are renegotiable.
  - Avoid direct suggestions. Instead, ask questions such as:
    a. "Have you thought about …?"
    b. "What would happen if you did …?"
    c. "Would you be willing to consider …?"

7. Attain closure.

  - Get commitment to specific solutions. Review exactly what they will do — measurable behaviors.
  - Set up a follow-up meeting.

THREE TYPES OF CONSULTATION: IS IT DEVELOPMENTAL, REMEDIAL, OR CRISIS?

Consultations can be divided into three types. Unique characteristics of the first stage of consultation define each type. While change is possible at any time, developmental consultation generally has more core conditions, which contribute to effective change.

Developmental Consultation

Developmental consultation is the optimum consultation. There is no crisis situation. A major goal is to create a learning experience for the consultee, which transfers to the third parties. Developmental strategies include teacher and parent education groups, classroom guidance activities, and other opportunities for personal and professional growth. This is discussed in Chapters 5, 6, and 7.

Remedial Consultation

In remedial consultation, it is apparent that some crisis or extreme situation will occur unless steps are taken to prevent the crisis. Intervention strategies are devised with the intent to improve the situation, to avert the crisis.

Crisis Consultation

In crisis consultation, an extreme or emergency situation has occurred, and the consultant is asked to solve it. This is often limited to a "bandage" or "firehouse" approach. Stress levels may be high, and the willingness of the consultees may be either very high or very resistant. Legal incidents often create crisis consultations.

WHO IS BEING HELPED?

Consultation texts often differentiate between the consultee and the third party. In consultation, they state the third party is the one who is being helped. We do not endorse this approach. It is important to understand the true implications of this approach.

We do not believe the consultee is an immovable, inflexible individual through which suggestions to change the third party are delivered. If, consultation is to be effective, the consultee must look at the part he or she plays in the relationship with that third party. If there is little willingness to change, the chances of change in that third party are greatly reduced. Yet many teachers and parents come to the consultation relationship looking only for ways to change the third party. The consultee's attitude can be understood in the context of the theoretical approach outlined earlier in this book. A and B work to change C through changes initiated by B's beliefs and behaviors.

WHO INITIATES THE CONSULTATION?

Consultation is initiated either by (1) the consultant, (2) the consultee, or (3) someone else in the system. Self-initiated consultation (2) is perhaps the most desirable initiation. It suggests a high level of motivation and subsequent willingness to change. If the consultant makes the availability of consultation known, it may increase the number of these self-referrals.

Other-referred consultation (1 and 3) may be more difficult to initiate. The consultee does not yet know he or she is supposed to have this relationship. In this case, the consultant should have a general strategy for initiating the consultation.

In general, we suggest the consultant approach the situation as a listener, not as a deliverer of ultimate truths or responsibilities. It is more likely that a person will enter the consultation relationship when it is clear that the consultant, in fact, does listen and demonstrates empathy. Contrast "The principal said we should talk about the problems you've been having with Stephanie. When can we meet?" with this consultation overture: "How are things going this year?" The second approach may seem more vague, but in fact is an invitation to share experiences. The second approach is asking an open-ended question. Closed questions such as "When can we meet?" put people on the defensive.

This overture approach is particularly effective when you have a minimal prior relationship, such as with the parents of students. The initiation of consultation through a threatening, impersonal phone call is not likely to produce satisfying results. Letters, e-mail, and meetings at scheduled events are alternatives. Tone of voice, even in these written and scheduled alternatives, is a key ingredient for success.

THE IMPORTANCE OF LIFESTYLE

Whether consultants are working with parents or teachers or others in consultation, it is essential that the lifestyle of all participants is understood.

In Chapter 3, we discussed the importance of understanding the short-term goals of student misbehavior. It is equally important to understand the longer-term goals of behavior and misbehavior. This long-term movement and behavior is called a lifestyle, a set of learned and chosen beliefs about how to treat others in relationships. Dinkmeyer and Sperry (2000) define it as a basic orientation toward life; similar to a personality, character, or psyche.

The consultant should be aware of the value of this lifestyle concept in consultation as it affects the three parts of the consultation relationship: student, teacher (consultee), and consultant.

The lifestyle does not come out of any specific experience, but, instead, from the continual repetition of the approach (lifestyle) used to cope with the tasks of life. Each individual adopts strategies that facilitate his or her life plan. As these experiences confirm our anticipation, the style of life, or decisions, is confirmed. By age 6, a lifestyle is fully formed. Therefore, consultants inherently deal with the lifestyle of the consultee.

When a person is apparently behaving inappropriately, it is important to remember that the behavior does make sense to the *behaver.* Each of us interprets our own experiences, and our own experiences make sense to us. This idea has a profound impact when working in consultation relationships. Two parties are talking about the behavior of a third. There are three different sets of perceptions working at once. How does the behavior of the third party make sense to that person?

The consultant meets with a consultee about a student who becomes violent in class. Party A hears repeated incidents of threats and acting which are clearly out of line with discipline policies, yet no action has been taken by B. When getting confronted, B says, "You need to know her father left the family two months ago, her Mom works the second shift, and she's had to take care of her brother and sister." Person B is explaining C's classroom behaviors through environmental causation explanation. A and B would have to change C's family to create change in B and C's classroom if this belief is the foundation of the consultation.

The Lifestyle of the Student

The consultee often presents the student case with a series of anecdotes or behaviors. If we understand the unity or pattern to these incidents, we are uncovering the lifestyle. Focusing on one or two confusing incidents will not help. If we can make a statement about the movement of the student, we are identifying a lifestyle. For example, "Dean is often discouraged and therefore does not try very hard" may summarize a series of incidents and reflects his lifestyle, which is "I am not capable, life is a series of challenges I can't complete, therefore, I will not try to do any of them."

Knowledge of the child's style of life is important, but not essential. It is as effective to understand the short-term goals of misbehavior. Several incidents may not reveal a lifestyle, but will reveal a pattern of purposive behavior. In extreme situations, understanding the child's lifestyle can be helpful (this approach is discussed later in this chapter).

Consultee Lifestyles: Basic Perceptions

Everyone has a lifestyle. Understanding lifestyles is helpful in the consultation relationship. We have found that some consultants lack the theoretical basis for their consultation, much less a strong understanding of the Adlerian lifestyle approach. However, it is well within the range of all consultants, regardless of orientation, to have an understanding of lifestyles. The following lifestyle ideas are expressed as elementary beliefs with a corresponding representative statement from a parent:

- I must be in control ("When I get my hands on him, he won't be a problem in the classroom any more. This has gone on too long.").
- I must win ("I'm tired of fighting with him, so whatever ideas you have to beat his system is fine by me.").
- I am superior ("Who told you to call me? What right do you have to tell me how to raise my children?").
- I must be right ("I've found that my methods are working with him at home, so whatever happens at school isn't following my system.").
- I am entitled ("His father is away on military duty, and I'm home alone with three kids. It's all I can do to keep our heads above water.").
- I must be comfortable ("I don't care what you do with him at school, it's fine by me.").

The lifestyle of the teacher or consultee can be understood in the context of the consultation request. Dinkmeyer, McKay, and Dinkmeyer (2000) have identified five common beliefs that impair teachers' effectiveness with students:

- I must control.
- I am superior.
- I am entitled; you owe me.
- I must be perfect.
- I don't count; others are more important than I.

Each of these beliefs may express itself in specific teacher behaviors and the resultant student reactions. The teacher who believes in control will often report to the consultant situations in which the classroom is "hard to control." The following anecdote shows how lifestyle expresses itself consistently in all areas.

Mr. Dowling requested a meeting with a school counselor on a consultation basis. He first asked whether this would affect his annual job performance review, whether the principal would be notified, and whether he could terminate the consultation at his discretion. When these issues were resolved, the presenting problem was a lack of control and mutual respect in the eighth-grade classroom. Students were causing trouble, and Mr. Dowling was not sure how to control the situation.

Similar incidents could be presented to illustrate the beliefs of superiority, entitlement perfection, and feeling less than others. These are simply a shorthand way of expressing a direction the person usually heads through life. While heading in that direction, certain encounters are sure to follow, and they reflect the chosen direction or belief. One would expect to have dehydration challenges if headed through the desert, and mildew if moving through the rainforest. Lifestyle challenges are predictable and come with every consulting relationship. It is essential to remember that every lifestyle has its challenges and strengths.

The Consultant's Lifestyle

The lifestyle of the consultant is also a critical part of the consultation relationship. What do you bring to the consultation relationship?

Beliefs Common in Helping Relationships Several beliefs are often found in consultants. The following three beliefs are examined in detail and reflect some of the possible lifestyle combinations a consultant can bring to the relationship. As with all lifestyles, there are assets and liabilities.

Control Consultants who are interested in control may have assets as problem solvers and organizers and may be good at data collection. The effort or need to control, however, may present challenges when one considers the nature of the consultation relationship. If there are three parties involved, and only one other comes to the meetings, it is hard to control the third party from a distance. It may be a challenge to even control the A to B relationship.

Logic is often another strength of the control approach to lifestyle. The ability to identify misbehavior by going through the anecdotes, the feelings, the reactions, and student reactions may be easier to follow for this person. However, the emphasis on logic may be impeded by the relative lack of sensitivity to affect or feelings. If you are strong on control you may be able to identify the content in a person's statements, but it may be more challenging to identify an accurate feeling.

A major area of potential conflict for the control lifestyle is power. Because it is important to control, situations where one is not in control, or powerless, are the most challenging. Consultation provides many opportunities for consultees to be "out of control." For this person, the issue of giving control or power to the consultee is a major step in establishing the relationship.

Miss Medlock has taught for 22 years in the same building. She literally has the children of the children she taught years ago. From this perspective, she accurately states, "I don't understand how children today can be so disrespectful. When I began teaching, I was respected because I was a teacher. Now, it almost seems a game to see if they can get me angry!"

Control Summary: Strengths — Logic, problem solving, organized

Challenges: Identifying affect, power struggles

Perfection One of the relative strengths of this approach is the commitment to high standards. Expressions of this can be found in extensive reading, comprehensive publicity, and dedication to identifying new resources. Perfectionists have even been described as "type A" personalities, or "ash tray cleaners and pillow puffers." Behind this humorous description is a lifestyle dedicated to getting something exactly right. In a consultation relationship, there are many opportunities for things to go wrong.

A belief that mistakes are deadly, and therefore must be avoided at all costs, can cloud the consultant's view of the relationship. This perfectionistic approach may hamper the consultant's ability to make recommendations or accept progress by the consultee.

Mrs. Selby has worked with the consultant on three previous occasions. Progress has been made and there have been substantive changes in the classroom. When she comes to the fourth session, she is visibly discouraged: "Things were going so well, and today was just terrible. It seems I am back to square one." The consultant listened and worked with Mrs. Selby, helping her to realize that "setbacks" are part of human behavior and not indications of total failures. Mrs. Selby has high standards, and interpreted the most recent problems as the sum and total of the entire consultation experience.

Perfectionist Summary: Strengths — High standards, achievement oriented

Challenges: Unwilling to make mistakes; avoid at all costs

The Need to Please The helping professions have an abundance of individuals who live to please. They are sensitive to others' needs, tuned in to what others want. This can be both an asset and a liability.

The liability presents itself when the consultant does not say "no." The following example demonstrates this pitfall:

> Mrs. Parker was asked to serve as a consultant to a neighboring school district, as there were issues that prevented the local counselor from serving as a consultant. She agreed, and devoted an afternoon each week to this task. Once she began, it became clear that much work needed to be done. She began to set aside two afternoons a week, gave consultees her telephone number so she could be reached at other times, and offered to see many of the consultees' students on an individual basis. It became difficult to keep up with the work at her regular school, but she never said no to the commitment she made.

The last sentence of the example gives us the situation from Mrs. Parker's point of view; this was a commitment, and it would be letting people down if she pulled back. Whether true or not, it looked that way to this consultant.

Need to Please Summary: Strengths: Empathetic team player, sensitive to others

Challenges: Hard to say "no" or establish limits

The value of lifestyle as a consultation concept is wide ranging. Additional discussions of this concept are found in Dinkmeyer and Sperry (2000).

THE TEACHER AS RESOURCE

If the consultant has a prior relationship with teachers, consultation can be clouded by these perceptions. For example, a school counselor can be a consultant. But prior to this relationship, the counselor has been disciplinarian, in-service chair, or referral resource for individual parent or student problems. These roles establish a perception in the minds of the teachers.

Some teachers enter the consultation relationship passively, waiting for the consultant to solve the problem. The teacher is a critical resource in consultation, not incidental to the problem situation. The consultant must see the teacher's role in the total situation. From this awareness comes the possibility of change.

The teacher brings assets to the consultation situation. A detailed picture of the interaction between the teacher and the child is an asset. The teacher is in the classroom where the interactions are occurring and provides the consultant with a perception of the causal factors. The consultant must be aware of how the teacher sees the problem. The teacher is also the only one who can provide feedback to the consultant regarding the effectiveness of the recommendations.

Teachers are essential resources in the consultation process. If the consultant believes effective relationships consist of questions followed by answers, this resource is also lost. If the teacher believes a consultation relationship is a referral for "repair," this resource is also lost. This chapter now moves to the key elements in an effective consultation relationship.

THE HELPING RELATIONSHIP

Consider the nature of the helping relationship. Perhaps the most extensive study of the helping professions was by Arthur Combs and his colleagues at the University of Florida (1969). Research by Combs indicates that the basic tool of the helper is the *self*.

The helping professions are based upon the capacity of the helper to be a problem-solving person. Helpers are able to dialogue with immediate, not delayed, responses. Communication and human relations skills that process dialogue instantly and meaningfully are at the core of the consulting process. The consultant must be able to listen to the whole message (cognitive–affective) and facilitate the potential of the consultee.

Teachers present problems from their own point of view. Typical responses arise from values, beliefs, purposes, and perceptions. The teacher may be aware of this belief system, but more often, it is not in immediate awareness.

The teacher functions on the basis of the current perceptions. If Belinda, a high school junior, behaves a certain way out of "meanness," then Belinda is treated as if she were mean. The consultant helps the teacher to develop alternative perceptions and become aware of resources to develop new methods of interacting and responding. The consultant facilitates perception change by relating to the consultee a perception of her beliefs and attitudes. This facilitative confrontation creates awareness, insight, and the opportunity to change beliefs and perceptions. Belinda can be more than a mean student when the consultation uses a holistic approach.

The consultant increases the consultee's understanding and acceptance of new hypotheses and new perceptions, or to make new information available to the consultee. The consultant helps to generate tentative hypotheses and explore alternatives.

We believe behavior is always understood as a consequence of perceptions about the world and self. If one is familiar with the history of the helping professions in the fields of counseling, psychology, and social work, it is apparent that they have frequently tried to change the behavior of significant adults by providing them with additional information. This has traditionally occurred in in-service programs, which present new theories, additional observations, or the results of research related to human behavior. For most teachers, this type of approach remains on the periphery of their consciousness. They hear about new ideas, they even consider them as exciting, possible, or plausible, but they do not make an attempt to change. Why? Knowledge alone does not produce a change in behavior. Knowledge is experienced in terms of its personal meaning. If knowledge is presented in a manner that involves the teacher's feelings and attitudes as well as cognitive acceptance, it can be meaningful for the teacher.

The teacher cannot hear about a new approach and be expected to change. This approach is considered in light of present perceptions, beliefs, and attitudes. If we help the teacher explore what might prevent the use of this approach, we affect the teacher–student interactions.

In consultation, the problem is compounded. Our beliefs (our lifestyle) have an organizing or directing effect on all of our perceptions. Established beliefs can limit the ability to change behaviors. Consulting means becoming concerned with the internal frame of reference of the teacher, child, and consultant. Emphasis on the importance of understanding the child's perceptual field is part of the process. There is an exaggerated emphasis that states, "If the teacher understood the child's perceptions, things would change." This understanding by itself will not bring about change.

In the training of helping professionals we strive to become more people oriented and less thing oriented. Consultants need to be more concerned about their relationship with the teachers and less concerned with the technical aspects of diagnosis. The consultant must value the teacher, communicating the teacher is a person of worth who is truly concerned with improving the present situation.

This relationship is contrasted with an attitude of professional superiority. Consultants often convey indirectly or nonverbally the message, "Teachers don't understand children," or other attitudes that devalue and degrade teachers. An effective helper always begins by seeing persons in a positive way, as dependable and capable. The consultant and consultee are equal collaborators in bringing about change.

The Combs study indicates that two characteristics stand out in terms of the helper's perceptions of self. Effective helpers appear: (1) to see themselves as identified and involved with persons, and (2) to have a positive view of self. Combs et al. (1969) suggest why these characteristics are important when they state:

> A positive view of self provides the kind of internal security which makes it possible for persons who possess such views of self to behave with much more assurance, dignity, and straightforwardness. With a firm base of operations to work from, such persons can be much more daring and creative in respect to their approach to the world and more able to give of themselves to others as well. (p. 74)

The person who is confident, spontaneous, and creative in the approach to problem solving communicates these values to the teacher. For example, the consultant is worthy, but does not have to be perfect. Consultants refuse to accept or participate in any myth that assumes the teacher will provide the problem and the consultant provides the solution. Combs et al. (1969) suggest:

> The question of methods in the helping professions is not a matter of adopting the "right" method, but a question of the helper discovering the right method for him. That is to say, the crucial question is not "what" method, but the "fit" of the method, its appropriateness to the self of the helper, to his purposes, his subjects, the situation, and so forth. We now believe the important distinction between the good and poor helper with respect to methods is not a matter of his perceptions of methods, per se, but the authenticity of whatever methods he uses. (p. 75)

This research has considerable implication for the type of person the consultant must be and the nature of the helping relationship. The consultant has an impact with abilities to deal with the internal frame of reference and uniqueness of each consultee. The consultant considers the uniqueness of the child, the teacher, the setting, and the relationships produced in this set of transactions, thereby facilitating growth in all of these areas. Arthur Combs was a pioneer in the helping professions. His work gives us a foundation that merges with the Individual Psychology approach.

A major problem of ineffective helpers is inauthentic or contrived methods, "put on" for a certain situation. This is communicated to the teacher as incongruent and confusing. Teachers are seldom convinced by someone who suggests the importance of listening, understanding, and accepting the child, but who demonstrates in the consultant relationship failure to listen, understand, and or accept others.

To summarize Combs's research, there is a significant difference between effective and ineffective helpers in the following dimensions. Effective helpers are characterized by the following perceptual organization:

A. The general frame of reference of effective teachers tends to be one which emphasizes:
   1. An internal rather than an external frame of reference.
   2. Concern with people rather than things.
   3. Concern with perceptual meanings rather than facts and events.
   4. An immediate rather than a historical view of causes of behavior.

B. Effective teachers tend to perceive other people and their behavior as:
   1. Able rather than unable.
   2. Friendly rather than unfriendly.
   3. Worthy rather than unworthy.
   4. Internally rather than externally motivated.
   5. Dependable rather than undependable.
   6. Helpful rather than hindering.

C. Effective teachers tend to perceive themselves as:
   1. With people rather than apart from people.
   2. Able rather than unable.
   3. Dependable rather than undependable.
   4. Worthy rather than unworthy.
   5. Wanted rather than unwanted.

D. Effective teachers tend to perceive the task as:
   1. Freeing rather than controlling.
   2. Larger rather than smaller.
   3. Revealing rather than concealing.
   4. Involved rather than uninvolved.
   5. Encouraging process rather than achieving goals
   (Combs et al., 1969, pp. 32–33)

Combs was a pioneer in understanding perceptions within school systems. In one of his last publications, he stresses the need for change: "powerful communication and feedback require collaboration among all stakeholders. The culture of schools, however, fosters isolation and individualism. Some schools are changing; but cultures die long, hard deaths" (Combs et al., 1969, p. 12).

CREATING A STRUCTURE FOR EFFECTIVE CONSULTATION

How does the consultant create visibility for consultation opportunities?

1. Faculty meetings, newsletters, e-mails, and personal visitations are opportunities for the entire staff to become aware of the services the consultant can provide.
2. Availability and accessibility at teacher locations and schedule flexibility to respond to requests for assistance.
3. Discussions with the administrator to elicit support for the consultation role.

The best methods for consulting will always depend upon the individuals and the setting. The consultant establishes a procedure that makes consultation visible and readily accessible. Dialogue with the administration helps the system. The administrator's attitude toward consultation is essential. Without administration support, consulting efforts often fail.

Consultation exists in an atmosphere where "deficiencies" in relationships are discussed. One must be cautious about procedures in which the teacher indicates to the administration the consultation request. Some administrators recognize that consultation is effective when the teacher talks with a person who has no supervisory or administrative responsibility over his professional position.

In summary, consultants must have:

1. Administrative support.
2. Freedom for teachers to seek consultation without administrative supervision.
3. Administrators do not serve as consultants. The consultant is available by being around places where teachers gather before school, during recess, and after school. This may not be the best setting to share concerns and problems. Thus, a schedule has office hours and flexibility to accept requests.

Although we stress a systems approach, the efficiency of individual consultation can be established. In this chapter the emphasis is on individuals, although in later chapters we discuss group methods.

Previous discussions have established conditions in which individual consultation is advisable. Fuqua and Newman (1985) list five conditions, which we amplify with our comments:

1. *Problems are strictly of an individual nature.* This is often the case when a teacher reports problems with a student.
2. *System interventions are impractical, unlikely, or untimely.* Consultants may be in systems where few seek their services. The system atmosphere may not be conducive to change.
3. *Problem perceptions are limited to individuals.* This is similar to item 1.
4. *The consultee's work setting is highly resistant to change.* This is similar to 2.
5. *Individual change may be more efficient than system-wide change.*

Regardless of the conditions, consultation on an individual basis can be effective.

THE DIAGNOSTIC STUDENT INTERVIEW

One secondary element of the consultation process may be a brief interview with a student. This interview is not lengthy. The purpose is to establish some impressions about how the student sees the world. It also enables the consultant to check tentative hypotheses. It always follows a consultation with the teacher.

This interview gathers information and checks impressions. It does not have therapeutic intentions. The consultant conveys to the student interest in the student and his or her progress in school. The student can talk about self and his or her relationship with the teacher, peers, and school tasks.

The interview is structured to understand the child's perceptions. Skilled consultants obtain insight into the lifestyle. Thus, although we provide suggested topics or questions, the interviewer will be free in the sense that the answers or responses will provide clues as to the most productive areas for investigation.

Some questions that have been found to be particularly useful include:

1. Which of your brothers or sisters behaves most like you? How?

2. Which of your brothers or sisters behaves most differently from you? How? (These questions provide some insight into how the child sees his or her behavior. They give some understanding of the child's perceptual field. By telling how his or her siblings are alike or different by implication, the child is telling a good deal about him- or herself.)

3. What do you like about school? Why?

4. What do you dislike about school? Why?

5. Are there any subjects you particularly like or dislike? (These questions provide some insight into how the child perceives school and its requirements.)

6. What do you particularly enjoy doing with mother or father? Why? When you misbehave, who disciplines you, mother or father? How?

7. What do you like to do least with mother or father? Why?

8. Do you have jobs to do at home? Do you usually do them without being reminded? (These questions provide some insight into the family atmosphere and the type of relationship that exists in the home.)

9. How do you spend your time when you can do just as you please?

If the relationship with the child is a good one — if he or she is interested and involved in the interview — sometimes additional diagnostic clues can be obtained by asking the following questions:

1. If you were going to be in a play or show, what kind of person would you like to pretend to be? Why?

2. If you were going to pretend to be an animal what animal would you like to be? Why?

3. Which kind of animal would you not like to be? Why?

4. If you had three wishes, and only three, what would you wish for first, second, and third?

These kinds of questions will give some insight into the fantasy life and wishes of the child. The kind of person may not be significant, but the *reasons* for the choice may provide some clues. One must determine why the person is chosen. For example, if he or she chooses to pretend to be a police officer, we don't know anything about the value structure, but if the child chooses a police officer because he or she would like to boss others around, instead of helping others, it gives us some idea of the value structure.

The selection of an animal also attains significance only after we have ascertained the reason. A child may choose to be an alligator, but we should not attempt to guess the reason. Some children may choose alligators because they are vicious and can "get even," while others choose them because they lie in the sun and sleep all day. The consultant must ask the child why he or she chose a particular animal in order to avoid projecting his or her own ideas upon the child. The kinds of wishes that are selected will also give some idea of how the child values people and things.

When the consultant has had special training in understanding the use of early recollections, these may be particularly useful in helping him or her gain an impression of the way in which the child views the world. When a child is asked to recall one of the first things he can remember happening to him, either before or after school or during his first years of school, these recollections provide some indication of his assumptions about life.

The following is an example of a particularly meaningful recollection taken from the case records of an 11-year-old child who was referred because, although he had an above average IQ, he seldom produced in the classroom in line with the teacher's expectations. The consultant asked, "Tell me about the first things you can recall that happened to you, and how you felt about them." The child replied, "I remember when I was 5, my friends could ride a two-wheeler, but I could only ride a tricycle. I tried to catch up to them but I couldn't. I felt very bad about this." Another recollection: "I would have to do all of my work over. My parents felt I was too small. I felt very unhappy." These recollections give us some insight into some faulty assumptions, such as:

- I am not as much as others my age.
- People don't believe I can function as well as I should.

The interview provides the consultant with an opportunity to establish some tentative hypotheses about the child's behavior. He or she attempts to ascertain the purpose of the behavior and uses this interview to pose some tentative hypotheses to the child, such as: "Could it be you are behaving the way you are because it keeps the teacher very busy with you?" "Is it possible you don't do your work in school so you can be excused from all requirements?" While the answers the child gives may be significant and are often an indication of an awareness of the reasons for his or her behavior, they are not all-determining. One must look closely for nonverbal signs such as tone of voice, nervous movement of the eyes, facial expressions, and of course, a roguish smile or twinkle of the eyes, which Dreikurs and Grey (1968) describe as the "recognition reflex."

ADDITIONAL SUGGESTIONS FOR CHANGE

The consultant must be well grounded in an understanding of the psychology of human behavior and the dynamics of classroom interaction. This enables the consultant to provide a variety of corrective techniques that can be tailored to the uniqueness of both the child and the teacher. Some general suggestions that have been found to be very helpful when applied ideographically include:

1. *Helping the teacher to be aware of the importance of his or her relationship with the child.* The consultant could suggest a specific way in which the teacher might change the relationship and indicate how this change, if it is done consistently, may influence the child. The encouragement or this relationship is basic to the consultation process.

2. *Helping the teacher to understand the efficacy of logical consequences, in contrast to punishment.* For example, the consultant can help the teacher to recognize that if the tardy child's assignment is <u>not</u> graded, the student may learn to come on time.

3. *Helping the teacher to avoid rewarding misbehavior.* Frequently, the teacher unconsciously helps to maintain the misbehavior. For example, if a child is acting up and disturbing the class, instead of removing the child, which may involve the teacher in a power struggle and may be just what the child is interested in, the teacher should refuse to fight with the student. Instead, the teacher might dismiss the child at this time and arrange a private session at a later date.

4. *Helping the teacher to be aware of the nature of his or her relationship with the children.* Some teachers are too kind, and the children run all over them. Other teachers try to be too firm and too tough, and the children only rebel. The consultant can provide the teacher with a more objective observation of the nature of his or her relationships with children. The consultant can help the consultee to see how each relationship must be composed of both kindness and firmness. The kindness will indicate to the children care and respect, while the firmness will indicate self-respect, which in turn elicits the children's respect.

5. *Helping the teacher to become aware of the power of the group and group discussion.* Since all behavior has a social purpose, behavior can often best be influenced through group discussion. The group can often serve as an excellent diagnostic tool. When the teacher does not know why the child is misbehaving during a group discussion, the consultant may ask the class, "Why do you think Johnny is acting as he is?" Frequently the peers will be very sensitive to the purpose of this misbehavior.

6. *Helping the teacher to become more aware of the way in which the child reveals lifestyle through interactions with others.* Nonverbal behavior (e.g., smiles, signals, and other facial expressions) may help the teacher see the child's psychological movement and the way in which he or she seeks to become significant in the group. It is only as the teacher becomes aware of each child's unique lifestyle that the teacher has access to procedures for modifying his or her behavior.

7. *Helping the teacher to recognize that one of the most powerful tools for change is the proper utilization of responsibility.* Too often teachers give responsibility to the child who has already demonstrated responsibility. It is much more useful therapeutically to give responsibility to a child who needs the responsibility to enhance development.

8. *Helping the teacher to be free from outmoded approaches for dealing with difficult children.* Teachers should be particularly cautious of using schoolwork or assignments as a punishment and should refuse to become involved in the client's attempts to manipulate the teacher. The teacher must become competent in understanding human behavior and motivation.

9. *Helping the teacher to understand the child's lifestyle and to learn to anticipate the child's actions.* Often when the teacher is confused, the best response is to do exactly the opposite of what the child expects.

10. *Helping the teacher to recognize that talking at the child will not change the behavior.* It is often observed that teachers tend to talk too much and act too little. The consultant should help the teacher to see how a new relationship and logical consequences are more efficacious.

11. *Helping the teacher to develop a classroom council.* When there is considerable difficulty within a room, a classroom council can help set limits and rules, which will be more acceptable to the total group.

TWO EXAMPLES OF INDIVIDUAL CONSULTATION

Individual consultation requires a number of skills and an awareness of procedures, but it is always based upon the capacity to develop an effective, problem-solving approach with the teacher. The following example illustrates some of the problems encountered in helping teachers to focus on the specific problem and to become aware of their feelings and reasons for behavior. Each of the consultant's carefully selected leads and responses has a specific purpose.

T = Teacher;   C = Consultant

C: Could you tell me something about this boy Phil?

T: Yes, he's in my eighth-grade science class, and he drives me insane.

C: He really bothers you. (*Hears the feeling.*)

T: The worst I've ever had.

C: Tell me about a specific time.

T: Every time I start to teach he gets up and walks around the room. Sometimes he just leaves the classroom.

C: Can you think of one specific incident recently that you could describe? (*Aims to get away from generalizations.*)

T: Yes, I was teaching science, and I thought I had a pretty good science lesson prepared. The boys and girls were sitting in a group when all of a sudden Phil starts to cough real loud. I thought maybe he needed to get a drink so I said, "Phil, if you want to get a drink, go ahead." He answered, "Oh no, that's OK." I proceeded to teach, when suddenly he just gets up and leaves my classroom. I asked him, "Where are you going?" He said, "I'm going to get a drink. You said I could." But this was 25 minutes later.

C: How did you feel when he did this? (*Attempts to see how behavior affects teacher.*)

T: I'm always angry whenever he does something like this. He really makes me mad.

C: What do you do? (*Attempts to identify teacher's response.*)

T: I told him to get back to his seat. Sometimes I try to ignore him.

C: When you tell him to go back, does he go right away?

T: Oh yes, he's usually pretty good. He might look out the window a few minutes, but he eventually strolls back to his place. I mean he's not bold or anything.

C: Do you have any idea why he does this? (*Investigates teacher's perception of purpose of behavior.*)

T: I think he does it to get my attention. He knows every time he walks around or leaves the classroom I'm going to stop whatever I'm doing and ask him, "What's wrong?" I think he's really a boy who craves attention. (*Here the teacher describes his home situation, stressing the fact that he has a very tough father.*)

C: What kind of attention do you give him?

T: Well, I try to spend time with him. I spend time after school. He's on the basketball team, and he's got tremendous potential, but he drives the coaches insane. He doesn't pay attention to what he's doing.

C: Could we just go back for a minute? You said that when he does this sort of thing you get really mad, and you also said at one point that you ignore him. What would you say is your usual reaction to what he does?

T: I think he's aware of the fact that he makes me mad.

C: Do you think he knows he's going to get you angry? (*Attempts to see how child perceives his response.*)

T: Well, I don't know if he can see my anger, because I don't ever really yell at him, or scream.

C: I was thinking that sometimes children, if they know they can get you angry, are really trying to control you. You know, they want to be in charge. (*Poses a tentative hypothesis so teacher can see the relationship between his feelings and child's purpose.*)

T: I really think he's a smart boy. He's got a high IQ, and I feel he could do much better in school. I'll give him five or ten science problems, and he'll do maybe two of them for homework. (She then describes his work on similar assignments.) I think he deliberately doesn't do the problems.

C: And you think he does this to get your attention?

T: Oh, I think so. If I keep him after school, he's really happy.

C: And yet the problem seems to be mostly in school. Are there ever times that you think that maybe you give him a little encouragement? (*Attempts to focus on school situation where teacher had problem.*)

T: I don't know, I think maybe I'm just very negative against him. I don't see him doing too many things I could praise him for. I can't praise him for burning a kid's hair, or leaving the room, etc. I could try that, though.

C: It would almost seem that if he wants attention, he could get it another way. He seems to want our attention. (*Creates awareness of how child gets attention.*)

T: I could maybe try looking for things. I don't know if I'll find anything, but I could at least try.

C: I think maybe for the next few days you should give it a try, even if it's just a small thing.

T: Yes, I really never thought of that. It might be what he needs.

C: If he could get your attention another way, he wouldn't have to resort to these other things.

In this example it appears that the child was involved in a power struggle with the teacher, but the consultant focused on attention getting as the purpose of misbehavior. The consultant's leads were appropriate, but the consultant could have caught the teacher's feeling of anger and explored the possibility of the child's desire to obtain power.

The following example illustrates how the consultant helps the consultee to explore her own beliefs:

T: I sent for you to get your help on my friend, Ricky.

C: Yes.

T: He appears to be a child who needs some kind of affirmation. He just slugs anybody, anytime, and then chuckles to himself. Basically he appears to be tenderhearted. I really like him a great deal. I want him to be accepted by the other kids. He really wants to be accepted, and it appears to me that he does all these things to get the attention he is looking for. Do you think that is correct, or am I beating at straws?

C: Do you mean that he wants to be accepted and doesn't know how to go about it? (*Clarifies teacher's belief.*)

T: Yes, to get this attention without using diabolical means.

C: Sure. Can you give me anything specific that he has done?

T: Somebody goes past his desk, and he takes a lunge at him, no matter who it might be.

C: How do you feel when this happens? (*Determines feeling in order to clarify purpose of behavior.*)

T: Well, I feel kind of sorry for the kid. I'd like to see him get along with the others. I've talked to others to see what the problem is, but they can't seem to pinpoint it. They want nothing to do with him.

C: Tell me more about how you feel.

T: I suppose basically I feel sympathetic toward him as he has so many good things about him. He really is tenderhearted. I would like him to be accepted. When we had our first parent-teacher-child conference, he was very quiet.

C: Did you tell the parents why he was so unpopular? (*Fails to explore teacher's belief about Ricky.*)

T: Yes. His mother was constantly at his defense. This greatly bothered me. The father didn't have much to say. The mother talked all the while. The father seemed to approve of my attitude. I felt I got nowhere with the mother. Later on we had another conference, this time only with the mother. She told me the father beats Ricky all the time. I began thinking his actions toward his peers might be revenge.

C: When he acts this way, what do the other children do? What are the consequences of his behavior?

T: They are varied. There's some laughter, girls feel defenseless, and boys generally ignore him or tolerate him. The girls complain when they have to sit near him.

C: How does he react when he hears these complaints? Does he look satisfied or happy? (*Tries to establish a purpose for action.*)

T: I think he is perplexed. Outwardly he shows little emotion.

C: Has he ever been mean to you? (*Clarifies idea about Ricky's behavior.*)

T: No, he never turns on me. I give him plenty to do.

C: From what you have said, he seems to tyrannize only those who are weaker than he is, more or less as his father does to him. I agree with you in thinking his goal is revenge. Do you ever punish him?

T: Sometimes if he is annoying someone near him, I move him away.

C: That really isn't a punishment, just a result of his action. Have you ever talked to him about this? (*Clarifies distinction between logical consequences and punishment.*)

T: I've said to him, "Tell me about how you act."

C: What did he say?

T: He wants to be accepted. He knows how he acts. Sometimes he says he doesn't know why he acts the way he does.

C: I'd like to make a few suggestions. On one of the better days, talk with him and hypothesize about revenge being the goal of his behavior. See what he says and what his reaction might be. See if you can encourage him as you have been doing. Make some observations, and we will discuss Ricky again in a week. What do you think you could do differently with him? (*Attempts to accomplish too much in one lead.*)

T: I guess I could start to be more aware of my feelings about him.

C: Your feelings, tell me more.

T: I really feel very angry at times, but it is only now that I've recognized it.

C: It's hard to admit this anger toward a child, but it will help us understand the interaction. Do you think you could find some small thing to encourage?

T: He is very helpful during math, and I could notice it.

Individual consulting involves putting counseling skills to use with the consultee to develop awareness, understanding, new relationships, and commitment to new procedures.

INDIVIDUAL CONSULTATION ON THE DVD

The DVD accompanying this text has four examples of individual consultation. For each example, there is a separate commentary track by the consultant. Appendix I is the transcript of the fourth example, "Ann Marie," a teacher concerned with a junior high student.

SUMMARY

Individual consultation requires skills similar to counseling. The consultant's attitude toward the consultee can be effective or ineffective. A structure for individual consultation requires prior efforts to create a comfortable atmosphere for referrals. Administration must play an important supportive but unobtrusive role.

REVIEW QUESTIONS

1. What is the difference between individual counseling and a consultation relationship?
2. Define differences between a crisis, remedial, and developmental consultation relationship.
3. What role does lifestyle play in consultation?
4. How can teachers be used as resources?
5. If counseling is a helping relationship, what do the authors mean when they state that consultation can also be a helping relationship?
6. What role does the diagnostic student interview play in consultation?

REFERENCES

Combs, A., Soper, D., Gooding, C., Benton, J., Jr., Dickman, J, & Usher, R. (1969). *Florida studies in the helping professions, monograph no. 37*. Gainesville: University of Florida Press.

Dinkmeyer, D., McKay, G., & Dinkmeyer, D., Jr. (2000). *Systematic training for effective teaching*. Coral Springs, FL: CMTI Press.

Dinkmeyer, D., Jr., & Sperry, L. (2000). *Counseling and psychotherapy: An integrated, individual psychology approach* (3rd ed.). Columbus, OH: Merrill.

Dreikurs, R., & Grey, L. (1968). *Logical consequences*. New York: Meredith Press.

Fuqua, F., & Newman, J. (1985). Individual consultation. *Counseling Psychologist, 13*(3), 390–395.

5

WORKING WITH TEACHERS

In this chapter, you will learn:

- the importance of teacher perceptions
- the fallacy of the useless triangle
- effective beliefs for teachers and consultants
- effective behaviors for teachers and consultants
- individual consultation techniques

The purpose of consultation with teachers is to identify faulty beliefs while offering alternative beliefs and corresponding behaviors for the teacher. If we can focus on beliefs, the behaviors will follow.

Consultation with teachers is the most challenging consultation relationship in the school. Administration and teacher consultation is an area that counselors report spending more time than "ideal" (Agresta, 2004). Although both real and ideal were less than 10% of a counselor's time, it joins academic scheduling and staff meetings as "more time spent than desired." School psychologists, in comparison, report consultation as the second most used professional role: assessment took almost half of their workday (40%), with consultation comprising 16% and counseling 6% of their time (Bramlett, Murphy, Johnson, & Wallingsford, 2002).

Teachers have a full schedule, including expectations for more effective discipline and higher test scores. Achievement through effective discipline, and all other available means, has become the primary job performance criteria for some teachers.

WHAT IS A GOOD TEACHER?

Much of a consultant's work is with teachers. Here are two points to consider about this population. A 1998 study of Tennessee teachers showed teachers have measurable effects on student achievement. This massive, statewide database has shown the effectiveness of the teacher as the major determinant of student academic progress. The study shows "teacher effects on student achievement have been found to be additive and cumulative, with little evidence that subsequent effective teachers can offset the ineffective ones" (Sanders & Horn, 1998, p. 247). Translated into consultation terms, we may be seeing students who are still being affected, negatively, by prior ineffective teachers.

The Hoover Institute (Goldhaber, 2002) has shown only 3% of teacher's influence on students can be attributed to measurable elements of the teacher (i.e., experience, education, number of years teaching). This means 97% of the influence on students comprises intangible elements such as enthusiasm and skill in conveying knowledge.

THE TEACHER-CONSULTANT RELATIONSHIP

The relationship between consultant and teacher is collaborative. Attention to the first stage of this relationship is crucial. Consulting involves understanding the dynamics of human behavior and the feelings, attitudes, and purposes of adults as well as children. It is important to be seen as a helping partner.

To establish this relationship, the consultant must be perceived by administrators as one who is available to help the significant adults, as well as the children. Many consultants schedule regular sessions with the school administrator. If the principal acknowledges and accepts the importance of a consultation relationship between counselor and teachers, a crucial first step in the process is achieved. The principal also must encourage these consultation relationships. The teacher can also be helped when the consultant recognizes the value of collaboration with family members (Amatea, Daniels, Brigman, & Vandiver, 2004).

The principal realizes that, in order to create this kind of role with staff, time is needed to establish the necessary and sufficient conditions for consultation. The consultant may spend the first month of the school year becoming acquainted with the administrators, teachers, and parents, both formally and informally. Consultants often schedule individual meetings with each teacher to find out how they can collaborate.

Consultants are listeners, becoming aware of perceptions of classrooms, students, and relationships. The consultant also identifies the strengths in the system.

A collaborative relationship with staff must precede all other efforts. The consultant must plan a daily schedule to avoid being continually manipulated by "the crisis situation." The real crisis is the need to develop a relationship with teachers that makes it both possible and probable that they will seek the consultant as a helper. One can easily be seduced into rapidly responding to every "crisis." However, this is usually highly unproductive.

Cultivating a positive relationship with teachers includes the following suggestions. Be accessible and go to the areas where teachers are usually found, such as the teachers' lounge. The teachers' lounge is not the place to conduct professional consultation. However, it may be the place where one can break down the artificial barriers that sometimes exist between the specialist and the teacher. Consultants share the professional concerns of teachers. Consultation can sometimes be seen only as child advocacy. Instead, what must be apparent to teachers is that the consultation helps the teacher to accomplish his or her responsibilities with less personal stress and tension.

Too often the consultant is seen as someone who suggests that the teacher's procedures are ineffective, followed by generalized advice, such as treat the child as an individual or provide more attention or love. Teachers often feel that little, if any, understanding is shown of problems when both the size of the class and available materials make this impossible.

The consultant must be able to enter the perceptual field of the teacher, to understand the teacher's frame of reference. Teacher beliefs such as "I must be in control" or "I know what is best for children" may be major deterrents to the change process. We shorthand this as POV (point of view).

Errors in Establishing the Relationship

A second-grade teacher comes to the consultant asking for help with Ryan, an active boy who is continually disrupting quiet work times.

T = Teacher   C = Consultant

T: Have you got any ideas about Ryan? He's really causing problems since school began, disrupting worksheet times.

C: Maybe you can isolate him — face his desk in the opposite direction.

T: I've tried that. He gets a big grin on his face and I feel that he's getting more attention!

In this example, what is the teacher's POV? The consultant is "seduced into the crisis" and first dispenses advice. The consultant has not heard the POV. The teacher's response gives large clues as to the purpose of Ryan's behavior, but the consultant missed this information while dispensing advice.

To empathize with a teacher in an inappropriate way is easily done, especially when the consultant has taught.

T: Have you got any ideas about Ryan? He's really causing problems since school began, disrupting worksheet times.

C: Yes, I used to have that problem when I taught fourth grade.

T: What did you do?

An attempt to empathize with the teacher may become an opportunity to dispense advice. No recognition of the current situation — the teacher's frame of reference — has been made. Consultants must ask, "Who is my client?" In almost all cases the answer should be, "My client is the person who brought me the problem." The consultant helps the consultee, who is the client, to recognize problem ownership. Though the consultee might like to "turn the case over" to the consultant, the consultant helps the consultee see her or his part in the interaction and create an awareness of the opportunity to change the problem situation. A more appropriate response would be:

T: Have you got any ideas about Ryan? He's really causing problems since school began, disrupting worksheet times.

C: You seem really bothered by Ryan. Can you give me a specific example where he did this recently? What would we hear and see?

The consultant does not operate as if the child were the one who is concerned about the problem. In many instances the student does not even think there is a problem! The client is the teacher.

In another case, the student, Jerome, seldom gets his arithmetic finished and spends the time talking with another child. This is not something he wants to change. When the teacher seeks a consultant about Jerome, an important point to recognize is that he does have a real problem. However, it may not be the same problem the teacher perceives. The problem that can be solved by the consultant and the teacher, working together, is the teacher's relationship with Jerome.

Another point that must be made clear is that one can only change his or her own behavior. If Jerome is to change, the teacher must change first. As the teacher functions differently, Jerome will begin to change. This does not imply that the teacher is at fault. Instead, it merely deals with the reality that the teacher must first change if the child is to change.

This strategy recognizes that the teacher is in discomfort, experiencing dissonance, and is therefore ready to change. This approach utilizes concepts of systems theory and realizes change in one part of the system impacts all other parts. Change involves changing both the teacher's and the child's perceptions.

Methods for communicating consultation opportunities are also changing. Distributing a newsletter has been an effective method to provide an opportunity for in-service contact with faculty. This newsletter could include material about identifying emotional problems, detecting guidance needs, implementing group discussion procedures, handling discipline, or conducting parent interviews. E-mail is also emerging as a viable method for publicizing and processing consultations (Kruger et al., 2001).

DISCIPLINE: THE USELESS TRIANGLE

A study by Don Dinkmeyer, Jr. (1980) has shown that teachers believe parents are the major cause of discipline problems in their classrooms. The research examined teacher perceptions of discipline problems. Most teachers agreed that discipline (behavioral) problems were present in their classrooms; those unacceptable behaviors that they had been unable to change. Further, these teachers saw this student–teacher relationship problem as being caused by the parent, poor home environment, or other external factors.

This belief appears to put a third corner, or triangular, framework on the discipline problem. If you believed that parents caused Jessica's behavior problems, what would you do? Telephoning her parents is certainly consistent with your belief. And this is exactly what teachers in Dinkmeyer's research reported — repeated attempts to contact parents, hoping they would own part of the problem. An important point is to recognize how consistent this teacher behavior is with the current belief and how one's beliefs influence behaviors.

If the teacher cannot effect change by parent contact, the teacher may turn to another adult — the school counselor, school psychologist, or principal. Teachers refer students to any other responsible adult, hoping for change. The teacher's behaviors express a bankruptcy of effective ideas with students on disciplinary matters. This referral has an explicit "fix the child" message that counselors, psychologists, or principals may be unable to achieve.

Teachers may express the following POV faulty beliefs when referring students:

1. The child is the problem;
2. The parent, counselor, psychologist, or principal can fix the problem; and
3. The teacher has no or a limited part in this repair process, so
4. Parents must fix the classroom problem.

When teachers ignore their own part in the disciplinary process, they also ignore part of the child when dealing with academic achievement.

TEACHER BELIEFS

The influence of the teacher's beliefs about self and the students cannot be overemphasized. If a student is in a classroom, the influences of the teacher's beliefs are inescapable. Consider the following example:

> Janice began the second grade in Mr. Bowman's classroom with new clothes, pencils, and an eagerness to learn. However, Janice's older brother, now in the fourth grade, also had been in Mr. Bowman's class. He was a bright and capable child, able to keep up with all work. One month into the school year, Janice was having trouble in her reading group. She was struggling with certain concepts and was becoming discouraged. Mr. Bowman said to Janice, "I'm sure you'll do well, because your brother was one of my best students."

What does Janice conclude from Mr. Bowman's remarks? What does Mr. Bowman believe about her? Was this encouraging or discouraging? The intentions were good but the method did not achieve the desired result.

Understanding teacher beliefs is essential. We must understand that each teacher has a set of beliefs that is the basis for behaviors in the classroom. Some of the beliefs are effective, enhancing the teacher–student relationship, and the ability of the students to grow and learn. Other beliefs are detrimental, causing relationship problems with students. We can examine some of the common faulty beliefs of teachers so we can recognize their implications for the consultation relationship. The common faulty teacher beliefs have been presented in Dinkmeyer, McKay, and Dinkmeyer (2000):

1. Students must cooperate with me.

   Implication: I am in charge; students will do what I say. If they do not, I am not an effective disciplinarian. Cooperation is based on my terms and means compliance with my needs.

2. I must be capable of handling all students and all situations, or I am not a good teacher.

   Implication: I must handle all students with the skills I now have. I have learned everything about handling students. A consultation relationship is an indication of failure.

3. My plans must succeed at all costs.

   Implication: My plan is the only one; no room exists for give and take in the relationship. To be in control or to "win" in challenges with my students is important. I have little flexibility in my relationships with others.

4. Some students are naturally bad and must be punished when they fail to cooperate.

   Implication: Not all students are good; some have no hope of correction. My approach is to use punishment as the discipline system to create compliance. The only discipline system that is effective is based on controls from outside the child.

5. I must control the classroom and all students so they do not control me. To be out of control is dangerous.

   Implication: To be in control is important. This concern is based on a real issue: How do I effectively handle a room of 30 or more students? Recognize that many teachers have not had extensive training in classroom management techniques. Others have been taught discipline systems, which emphasize control as the primary technique.

6. Unhappiness is externally caused, and I have no ability to control or influence my feelings.

   Implication: I cannot expect to change the present situation. For me to change has no "payoff." I have no resources to help me change.

7. Children are the product of their heredity and the larger environment and cannot be changed.

   Implication: The student cannot be influenced by any of my actions or beliefs. The influence of the school is minimal.

Teachers will frequently present one or more of these beliefs to the consultant. A teacher is unlikely to say, "I must be in control," but his or her actions and words will be consistent with this belief. See Table 5.1 for a summary of how beliefs affect a teacher's behavior.

TABLE 5.1 Ineffective and Effective Characteristics of Teachers

Ineffective Characteristics		
Teacher's Belief	**Teacher's Behavior**	**Results for Students**
I must control.	Demands obedience. Reward and punishes. Tries to win. Insists is right and students wrong. Overprotects.	Rebel: must win or be right. Hide true feelings. Seek revenge. Feel life is unfair. Give up. Evade, lie, steal. Lack self-discipline.
I am superior.	Pities students. Takes responsibility. Overprotects. Acts self-righteous. Shames students.	Learn to pity selves and blame others. Criticize others. Feel life is unfair. Become dependent. Feel need to be superior.
I am entitled. You owe me.	Is overconcerned with fairness. Gives with strings attached.	Don't trust others. Feel life is unfair. Feel exploited. Learn to exploit others.
I must be perfect.	Demands perfection from all. Finds fault. Is overconcerned about what others think. Pushes students to make self look good.	Believe they are never good enough. Become perfectionists. Feel discouraged. Worry about others' opinions.
I don't count. Others are more important than I.	Is permissive. Sets no guidelines. Gives in to students' demands. Feels guilty about saying no.	Expect to get own way. Are confused. Do not respect rights of others. Selfish.
Effective Characteristics		
Teacher's Belief	**Teacher's Behavior**	**Results for Students**
I believe students can make decisions.	Permits choices. Encourages.	Feel self-confident. Try. Contribute. Solve problems. Become resourceful.

(Continued)

TABLE 5.1 Ineffective and Effective Characteristics of Teachers (*Continued*)

Effective Characteristics		
Teacher's Belief	**Teacher's Behavior**	**Results for Students**
I am equal, not more or less than others.	Believes in and respects students. Encourages independence Gives choices and responsibility. Expects students to contribute.	Develop self-reliance, independence, responsibility. Learn to make decisions. Respect selves and others. Believe in equality.
I believe in mutual respect.	Promotes equality. Encourages mutual respect. Avoids promoting guilt feelings.	Respect selves and others. Have increased social interest. Trust others.
I am human; I have the "courage to be imperfect."	Sets realistic standards. Focuses on strengths. Encourages. Is not concerned with own image. Is patient.	Focus on task at hand, not on self-elevation. See mistakes as challenges. Have courage to try new experiences. Are tolerant of others.
I believe all people are important, including myself.	Encourages mutual respect. Invites contributions. Refuses to be "doormat." Knows when to set limits and say no.	Know and accept limits. Respect rights of others.

Source: Don Dinkmeyer, Gary D. McKay, and Don Dinkmeyer, Jr., *Systematic Training for Effective Teaching (STET): Teacher's Handbook*. CMTI Press, © 2000. Reproduced with permission. All rights reserved.

The role of the consultant is to listen carefully to all consultee statements for the underlying beliefs. Recognize that teachers often begin by focusing on changing the student. While listening is important, this is not the place to begin the consultation relationship. Certain procedures must be utilized to stimulate recognition of beliefs, offer alternative beliefs and behaviors, and create an atmosphere conducive to this recognition, presentation, and change.

INDIVIDUAL CONSULTATION

Teachers frequently present requests on an individual basis. It is rare to have two or more teachers approach the consultant about a similar situation. Each request often focuses on one student. Even in team-teaching situations, one of the team members usually represents the team.

The consultant might therefore see a need to work with teachers on a one-to-one basis. Individual teacher consultation can be hampered by several considerations:

1. *Advice-giving seems an immediate, if not natural response.* The tendency is for consultants to hear feelings, beliefs, and explore alternatives with students. But with teachers, we give advice. The answer-machine approach, hoping to produce simple solutions by prescription, often ignores the feelings, beliefs, and alternatives for each teacher. The consultant as merely an advice-giver is an outdated, ineffective professional resource.

2. *One cannot consult effectively unless the internal frame of reference of the consultee is understood.* It is vital that the perceptions and beliefs be identified and examined. In an individual consultation relationship, this examination is limited by the consultee's willingness to expose these beliefs with the individual consultant.

3. *Individual consultation presents opportunities for the teacher to respond to ideas* with comments such as "That doesn't work," "I've already tried that," or "When were you last in a classroom?" Consultant suggestions may be blocked when the teacher has no peers offering feedback.

4. *Consultants are limited to their own resources — their education, experiences, and ideas.* These limited resources never embrace all types of situations teachers will present. If the teacher is in a group of peers, the disadvantages of the consultant's expertise can be minimized.

Working with teachers in groups is an effective, underused vehicle for consultation and education. Unless one is aware of the potential benefits of didactic-experiential group, consultation with teachers can be a discouraging, limited experience. Therefore, teacher groups can be established for both problem solving and educational purposes. Teacher education coursework does not completely prepare individuals for the classroom. Perhaps less than one-third of those who receive teacher certification have any coursework in groups. If a teacher is not aware of group forces, dynamics, and opportunities to influence her or his groups, a basic, missing link is in the educational process for our educators. Failing to cover basic concepts such as group dynamics undereducates our teachers. See Appendix II for an example of a teacher group.

TEACHER EDUCATION IN-SERVICE COMPONENTS

Teacher in-service training must go beyond the single day in August that includes outside speakers or time provided for organizing the classroom. The skills needed by teachers require a consistent approach to acquiring these skills throughout the year. A comprehensive approach to teacher in-service involves the use of *Systematic Training for Effective Teaching* (STET) (Dinkmeyer et al., 2000). STET topics include understanding behavior and misbehavior, understanding yourself as a teacher, encouragement, communication and listening, expressing your ideas and feelings to students, exploring alternatives and problem-solving discussion, promoting responsible behavior through natural and logical consequences, applying natural and logical consequences, understanding the group, group leadership skills, group guidance, group class meetings, understanding and dealing with special problems, and working with parents. The STET program can be taught in a comparatively short 1-hour-per-session format or a more thorough 2-hour format.

The STET approach divides each session into a learning cycle with three major components. In the first part, new ideas are presented through the reading and charts. These ideas become skills that are practiced in the teacher group through audio incidents and written problem situations. The third part is applications; ways to use the ideas with students. STET is based upon the importance of applying the democratic process to the educational experience and must be taught in a manner that models the principles and procedures it advocates.

Essential Topics for an In-Service Program

An effective program needs to include the following topics:

1. A useful, pragmatic theory of human behavior
2. Motivation techniques
3. Communication skills
4. Discipline techniques
5. Working with groups
6. Working with parents

A Useful, Pragmatic Theory of Human Behavior

How does the student operate in the classroom? Many teachers do not have an effective understanding of themselves and their students. The result is often confusion. Human behavior is usually predictable. In Chapter 3, the Adlerian approach to human behavior was presented, which gives teachers a better understanding of the students in the classroom. In particular, the four goals of misbehavior are an illuminating concept. It allows teachers to accurately understand and react to students.

An equally important aspect of human behavior is understanding ourselves. In the consultation relationship, this information is difficult if not impossible to present in a one-to-one setting. Instead, information on human behavior and self-understanding stands a greater chance of acceptance when presented in a group and educational setting. Individual Psychology is continuing to make inroads with other approaches, such as reality therapy, when working with teachers (Glasser & Carlson, in press).

Motivation Techniques

Many students who require the most motivation do not receive any, and those requiring the least receive the most motivation. When a praise and reward system is created, the least motivated are left behind. Additional motivation techniques such as encouragement can be taught and practiced in the group.

Communication Skills

Few people are naturally good listeners. How can we listen to students? Traditional teacher roles may not recognize the importance of listening to students as a motivation skill. When students are heard, they are more motivated. Essential communication skills for teachers include reflective listening, I-messages, and problem-solving conferences. The consultant models these skills while working with the teacher.

Discipline Techniques

Discipline often focuses on techniques for regaining control in the classroom. Effective discipline procedures are preventive. Time-out and referrals to principals or counselors do not make a totally effective discipline system.

Most teachers are familiar with punishment-based discipline systems. A system based on natural and logical consequences is an alternative. Each choice for the student is a learning process. Even if the "wrong" behavior occurs, the student learns from this choice.

Working with Groups

Teachers receive little or no education in group dynamics. Group dynamics explain the individual goals of misbehavior. All students always seek to belong within the group: an individual's goals of misbehavior and appropriate behavior occur within the group setting and dynamics.

The group context of behavior and misbehavior, group dynamics, group leadership skills, classroom group guidance, and classroom meetings are essential teaching skills. Because teachers may not have any previous education in these group areas, consultation education might begin with any of these principles.

Working with Parents

Effective consultation procedures with parents are fully discussed in Chapter 7. Perhaps the most rapid shift within our society is occurring within the family. Fewer than half the children born today will grow up within an "intact" (two continuously married parents) family.

The consultant cannot ignore the parents, nor can we neglect the opportunity to teach teachers how to deal with parents.

RATIONALE FOR PROBLEM-SOLVING GROUPS

Working with teachers in education groups helps the consultation process. Teachers have a new core of information, skills, and self-awareness. These assets are efficiently transmitted in education groups. Once teachers acquire this baseline, consultation for problem solving can begin.

Working with teachers in groups is more meaningful when the consultant recognizes that we are indivisible, social, decision-making beings whose actions have a social purpose. This view of teachers and students as social beings develops new awareness and gives meaning to all verbal and nonverbal interactions. It is a comprehensive understanding of human thought and behavior.

In a group, teachers can become more aware of their traditional methods of responding to difficult children. The group setting provides a new way to see the lifestyle, faulty assumptions, and mistaken ideas of both student and teacher. It is essentially a holistic approach. The group setting takes into consideration not only the intellect, feelings, and behavior of the child, but also the teacher.

Groups create experiences for teachers in a supporting, caring, accepting atmosphere. The teacher has access to feedback about personal behavior, feelings, and attitudes, and through this, can develop a new perspective on relationships. Effective procedures for working with children can be discussed. The group also benefits teachers who do not have difficulties with children. It gives them an opportunity to share their successful techniques with another.

In order to understand group dynamics, teachers must experience being a group member. Often teacher education has not allowed teachers to have an experience either as a group member or a group leader.

If we are going to deal with the whole child, we must engage teachers by participation as "whole teachers."

Placing teachers in a group recognizes that most problems are interpersonal and social. The challenge that the teacher presents originated in a group interaction with the student. The teacher can become aware of the necessity of understanding behavior in its social context. The teacher group then has the opportunity to analyze the student's lifestyle. The student's unique approach to the tasks of life will be consistent with his or her self-concept and assumptions about life. More important, the consultant and the group have an opportunity to observe the teacher's lifestyle and the characteristic responses to students and members of the group.

The group setting provides the consultant and group members with an extremely valuable social laboratory. It is a miniature society or microcommunity that reflects the school's atmosphere. As the teacher learns to function as a member of the group, insights can be developed as to how the student functions in a group. Through this process, teachers are able to understand how they function in a group. The group has diagnostic, educational, and therapeutic values.

Behaviors can be observed in the group setting. Teachers cannot mask or bluff their way through a group of teens. The teacher's characteristic approach to working on problems is shared in the group setting.

A number of therapeutic effects can be processed in the group setting. The group provides the opportunity for a unique type of acceptance. This is a setting in which teachers can experience empathy from their peers. It also provides the opportunity to ventilate and express how they feel.

In the group, teachers try out ideas and process the feedback from other teachers in the group. Recognition that problems with children are universal, and that other teachers are experiencing the same challenges, occurs during the group. Universalization can help the group build trust, cooperation, and momentum. This can stimulate one's altruism and desire to help fellow professionals become more effective. Each member helps every other member.

The group provides teachers with an opportunity to hear other challenges and develop some ideas about how to handle a situation that, up to this point, they have not even encountered. Spectator therapy, learning from another's experience, is a major benefit. See Appendix II for an example of teacher consultation "C" groups.

THE ENCOURAGEMENT PROCESS

In the day-to-day activities of the classroom, the encouragement process can be a very effective means of reinforcement. Consultants model the encouragement process in direct work with teachers as well as teach these important concepts. Through careful planning and organization, the teacher then can use the encouragement process to help pupils.

The process of encouragement specifically involves:

- Valuing the individual child as is, not as reputation indicates nor as you hope will be — but as is.
- Showing faith in the individual child. This will help to develop a feeling of "can-ness" or a belief in self.
- Having faith in the child's ability. This enables the teacher to win the child's confidence while building his or her self-respect.
- Giving recognition for effort as well as a job well done.
- Using the group to help the child develop.
- Integrating the group so that the individual child can discover his or her place.
- Planning for success, assisting in the development of skills.
- Identifying and focusing on strengths and assets rather than mistakes.
- Using the individual's interests in order to motivate instruction. (Dinkmeyer et al., 2000)

Encouragement is a process, not a single effort. It lets the student know that the teacher believes in and will treat him or her with respect and trust. The student's value as a person is reflected in the teacher's attitude toward the student and the student's behaviors.

Encouragement should not be confused with praise, although both are efforts to motivate students. Praise puts the emphasis upon the product, while encouragement stresses the effort of contribution. (See Table 5.2.)

Dinkmeyer et al. (2000) outline the differences between praise and encouragement:

- Encouragement is helping students believe in themselves and in their abilities.
- Encouragement is a basic attitude toward yourself and other people.
- Encouragement is different from praise. Praise goes to those who excel or come in first; encouragement can be given for any positive movement. Encouragement does not have to be earned. (p. 64)

TABLE 5.2 Differences between Praise and Encouragement

Praise		
Underlying Characteristics	**Message Sent to Child**	**Possible Results**
Focus is on external control.	"You are worthwhile only when you do what I want."	Child learns to measure worth by ability to conform; or child rebels (views any form of cooperation as giving in).
Focus is on external evaluation.	"You cannot and should not be trusted." "To be worthwhile, you must please me." "Please me or perish."	Child learns to measure worth on how well he or she pleases others. Child learns to fear disapproval.
Rewards come only for well-done, completed tasks.	"To be worthwhile, you must meet my standards."	Child develops unrealistic standards and learns to measure worth by how closely he or she reaches perfection. Child learns to dread failure.
Focuses on self-evaluation and personal gain.	"You're the best. You must remain superior to others to be worthwhile."	Child learns to be over-competitive, to get ahead at the expense of others. Feels worthwhile only when "on top."

Encouragement		
Underlying Characteristics	**Message Sent to Child**	**Possible Results**
Focus is on child's ability to manage life constructively.	"I trust you to become responsible and independent."	Child learns courage to be imperfect and willingness to try. Child gains self-confidence and comes to feel responsible for own behavior.
Focus is on internal evaluation.	"How you feel about your-self and your own efforts is most important."	Child learns to evaluate own progress and to make own decisions.

(Continued)

TABLE 5.2 Differences between Praise and Encouragement (*Continued*)

	Encouragement	
Underlying Characteristics	**Message Sent to Child**	**Possible Results**
Recognizes effort and improvement.	"You don't have to be perfect. Effort and improvement are important."	Child learns to value efforts of self and others. Child develops desire to stay with tasks (persistence).
Focuses on assets, contributions, and appreciation.	"Your contribution counts. We function better with you. We appreciate what you have done."	Child learns to use talents and efforts for good of all, not only for personal gain. Child learns to feel glad for successes of others as well as own successes.

Source: J. Carlson and C. Thorpe, *The Growing Teacher* (Englewood Cliffs, NJ: Prentice Hall, Inc., 1984, 39–40). Reprinted by permission.

The differences between praise and encouragement are sometimes subtle. A teacher once described the differences between the two as follows: "Imagine your students are running a race. The cheering, prizes, and applause at the finish line are praise. Encouragement is what you do during the race."

Praise affects the child's self-image. The impression that personal worth depends upon how one measures up to the demands and values of others comes with praise. "If I am praised, my personal worth is high. If I am scolded, I am worthless." The ability to cope with challenges cannot depend on the opinions (positive or negative) of others.

Students may come to see praise as a right. Therefore, life is unfair if praise isn't received for every effort: "Poor me — no one appreciates me." Students may feel no obligation to perform if no praise is received. "What's in it for me? What will I get out of it? If no praise (reward) is forthcoming, why should I bother?" These students may be some of the highest achievers in the classroom, but they are "hooked on praise." Praise can be discouraging. If the student is not "praise-worthy," what can the teacher say to the student?

If a student has set high standards, praise may sound insincere. This is particularly true when efforts fail to measure up to personal standards. In such a student, praise only serves to increase anger and resentment at others for not understanding the disappointment.

In order to feel adequate, students must feel useful and know that their contributions count. Since motivation to learn and change manifests itself in terms of how people see themselves, those who teach and consult must become instruments of positive feedback. We can help teachers and students feel useful by identifying their talents and suggesting ways in which they might use these talents to make a contribution. A list of positive talents that could be recognized and encouraged is given in Table 5.3.

We help teachers and students believe in themselves by believing in them. We must communicate confidence and play down mistakes. We must be sensitive and alert to point out positive aspects of their efforts, recognizing improvement as well as final accomplishments.

HOW TO ENCOURAGE

The following points will be helpful to begin the encouragement process and motivate teachers and students:

- *Build on teachers' and students' strong points.* Look for positive efforts as well as results.
- *Minimize the teachers' or students' weak points.* Avoid nagging, criticizing, or spending an undue amount of time talking about what could have been done.

TABLE 5.3 Positive Traits to Use for Encouragement

friendly	aware	popular
highly regarded	anticipating	peaceful
thoughtful	strong	appealing
affectionate	sensitive	determined
well-liked	alert	sure
adored	keen	attractive
kind	content	untroubled
alive	comfortable	graceful
independent	relaxed	enthusiastic
capable	at ease	eager
happy	wide awake	optimistic
proud	worthy	joyful
gratified	admired	courageous
excited	sympathetic	hopeful
good	concerned	pleased
inspired	appreciated	excited
jolly	secure	interested
warm	glad	turned-on
caring	brave	intelligent

- *Tell teachers and/or students what you appreciate.* Some encouraging statements could be "I really enjoy seeing you smile" or "I like the neatness of your paper. It's such a pleasure to read" or "Thank you for turning in your assignment early. Now I have more time to spend on reading it before the avalanche of other papers hits."
- *Be friendly.* Take time to listen and show care and concern.
- *Demonstrate your liking for the teacher or student.* Such things as a personal comment, a special note, or an arm around the shoulder convey liking in a meaningful way. Spending time with students and teachers during and after class or after school hours also shows that you care.
- *Suggest small steps in doing a task.* The entire job may seem too overwhelming. Give discouraged teachers or students a small amount of work to do. As they finish each increment, they will feel encouraged.
- *Be humorous.* A wink, a pun, or a laugh at oneself can warm relationships. Always laugh with teachers and students, never at them.
- *Recognize effort.* Recognize attempts to do a task even though a job might not be well done. In initial stages of a new behavior or learning task, teachers and students need extra support and encouragement. Once they develop proficiency and begin to experience success, the secondary reinforcing property of the act itself takes over.
- *Become aware of the interaction between yourself and the student or teacher.* Realize that all behavior has a purpose and that often our responses are counterproductive. For example, when a student annoys us in an effort to gain our attention, we usually respond with a lecture on inappropriate behavior, scold, punish, or give some other form of attention. This attention actually supports the negative behavior rather than eliminating it.
- *Discipline students with fewer words.* Actions are more effective than words. Angry words are discouraging and often untrue. After taking firm action, resume talking with the student in a friendly manner, conveying the impression that you still and always will respect the student as important. The behavior is what is not acceptable.
- *Do not own the teachers' or students' problems.* Allowing teachers or students to solve their own problems indicates your faith in them, giving them flexibility and tending to their own concerns and interests.
- *Do not use rewards and punishments.* These procedures are discouraging and ineffective.

- *Accept teachers and students as they are*, not as you wish them to be.
- *Be understanding and empathic*. Look at the world from the teacher's or student's point of view.

THREE-STEP METHOD OF ENCOURAGEMENT

Step 1: Identify Positive Behaviors, Traits, and Efforts

Many educators have a difficult time identifying positive behavior. Table 5.4 offers some examples of behavior, along with the associated mental health principles. In order to motivate students, we must have a clear idea of what we would like to encourage and what we would like to see changed. Then we must indicate what this means in terms of behavior, including the required effort and movement.

Sometimes we think we are being helpful and guiding students in positive ways when in reality we are not. To be aware of the pitfalls of discouragement is very important.

Discouraging statements made *prior* to behavior include:

- Don't get dirty.
- Watch yourself.
- You aren't old enough.
- Be careful.
- Let me do it for you.
- Let me show you how.
- I know you can't do it.
- If younger children can do it, so can you.
- Look at how well Susie does it.

Discouraging statements made *after* the behavior include:

- No, that's not right.
- I shouldn't have trusted you.
- You could have done better.
- I've told you a thousand times.
- When will you become responsible?
- If you'd only listen to me.
- If only you weren't so lazy.
- You did it again.
- Oh, when will you learn?
- Don't you have any pride in your work?

TABLE 5.4 Positive Mental Health

Principle	Behaviors
Respects the rights of others.	Takes turns. Does not monopolize everyone's time. Cleans up supplies after an art lesson. Does not disturb other students who are working or concentrating on something.
Is tolerant of others.	Walks slowly so others can keep up. Waits quietly while others complete their assignments or tasks. Accepts all children and all abilities on the playground. Helps students from other cultures with English or comprehending school rules.
Is interested in others.	Includes/invites others to play. Shows concern for absent students. Volunteers to help others. Talks to and socializes with other students. Promotes or suggests social functions.
Cooperates with others.	Completes assignments on time. Works facilitatively in groups. Listens to what others say. Works with others rather than against them.
Is courageous.	Takes risks. Enjoys novel and different experiences. Is calm under pressure of tests. Acts enthusiastically toward challenges.
Has a true sense of self-worth.	Likes and validates himself. Acts in a realistic fashion. Understands and accepts his assets and liabilities. Has the courage to be imperfect.
Has a feeling of belonging.	Frequently mentions groups to which he belongs (e.g., friends, scouts, sports teams, church clubs). Feels accepted in school and does not need to act out to find his place. Makes a positive contribution to a group. Exercises a vote/voice in appropriate activities and procedures.

(*Continued*)

TABLE 5.4 Positive Mental Health (*Continued*)

Principle	Behaviors
Has socially acceptable goals.	Works within school rules.
	Is involved in the classroom.
	Cooperates with others and is just and fair.
	Doesn't precipitate fights and withdraws from physical conflict.
Puts forth genuine effort.	Tries hard on assignments.
	Does homework.
	Participates in discussions.
	Becomes absorbed and interested in learning.
Meets the needs of the situation.	Makes good decisions.
	Is able to solve problems.
	Handles spontaneous situations in a responsible manner.
	Does not under- or over-react to assignments.
Is willing to share rather than thinking, "How much can I get?"	Readily offers assistance to others.
	Shares lunch, pencils, crayons, etc.
	More process-oriented than outcome-oriented.
Thinks of "we" rather than just "I."	Uses words like "we," "us," and "our" rather than just "I," "me," and "mine."
	Shows caring and concern for others.
	Frequently offers to share.

Source: J. Carlson and C. Thorpe, *The Growing Teacher* (Englewood Cliffs, NJ: Prentice Hall, Inc., 1984, 34–35). Reproduced with permission.

The following list will be helpful in suggesting and identifying personality strengths in students.

1. *Special aptitudes.* Intuition. Making guesses that usually turn out right. Having a "green thumb." Mechanical or sales ability. Skill in construction or repairing things. Mathematical ability.
2. *Intellectual strengths.* Applying reasoning ability to problem solving. Intellectual curiosity. Thinking out ideas and expressing them orally or in writing. Openness to accepting new ideas. Original or creative thinking. The ability to enjoy learning.
3. *Education and training.* Any high grades. Improvement in grades. Scholastic honors. Vocational training or self-education through study and organized reading.
4. *Work.* Experience in a particular line of work. Job satisfaction, including enjoying one's work, getting along with co-workers, taking pride in job duties.

5. *Aesthetic strengths.* Recognizing and appreciating beauty in nature and the arts.
6. *Organizational strengths.* Demonstrating leadership abilities. Developing and planning short- and long-range goals. Ability in giving orders as well as in carrying them out.
7. *Hobbies and crafts, electronics.* Special interests and training in hobbies and crafts. Abilities in computer, video gaming, and similar electronic media.
8. *Expressive arts.* Dancing, writing, sketching, painting, sculpture, modeling with clay. Ability to improvise music or to play a musical instrument. Rhythmic ability.
9. *Health.* Good health represents a strength. Emphasis on maintaining or improving health through nutrition, exercise, and stress management.
10. *Sports and outdoor activities.* Active participation in outdoor activities and organized sports, camping, or hunting.
11. *Imaginative and creative strengths.* Using creativity and imagination for new and different ideas.
12. *Relationship strengths.* Ability to meet people easily and make them feel comfortable. Ability to communicate with strangers. Treating others with consideration, politeness, and respect. Being aware of the needs and feelings of others. Listening to what people are saying. Helping others to be aware of their strengths and abilities.
13. *Emotional strengths.* Ability to give and receive affection. Being able to feel a wide range of emotions. Being spontaneous. Ability to put oneself in other people's shoes.
14. *Other strengths.* Humor. Being able to laugh at oneself and take kidding. Liking to explore new horizons or try new ways. Willingness to take a risk with people and in situations. Perseverance. Having a strong desire to get things done and doing them. Ability to manage money. Knowledge of languages or different cultures through travel, study, or reading. Ability to make a public presentation. Making the best of one's appearance by means of good grooming and choice of clothes.

Step 2: Focus on the Specific Deed Rather Than the Doer

Although we may not approve of a student's behavior, she or he always deserves our respect as a person. No better motivation can be given than clearly identifying a student's positive behavior when she or he does things we like. Avoid making statements such as, "You are terrific (wonderful, super, lovable, etc.)." The problem with such comments is that the student may assume that the converse is also true — that when they do not please us, they must be terrible, worthless, unlovable. As we clearly point out what the student is doing that is positive, she or he will be encouraged and motivated. This concept is illustrated in Table 5.5.

Step 3: Implement by Using the Language of Encouragement

Teachers can maximize motivation by communicating clearly. Minimizing our own opinions and values and helping students grow to believe in themselves are the keys to success in the encouragement process.

Phrases that demonstrate belief in the student include:

- "I like the way you worked that problem through."
- "I like the way you dealt with that."
- "I'm glad that you enjoy reading."
- "I'm glad you're satisfied with the project."
- "Since you are not satisfied with the project, what do you think you can do so that you will be pleased with it?"
- "You look pleased."
- "How do you feel about it?"

Phrases that display assurance include:

- "You'll work it out."
- "I have confidence in your decision-making skills."
- "You'll finish it."
- "Wow, that's a tough one, but I'm sure you'll work it out."
- "Knowing you, I'm sure you'll do fine."

TABLE 5.5 Comparison of Focus on Doer and on Deed

Action	Focus on Doer	Focused on Deed
A student turns in a neat paper.	"You're wonderful!"	"I really like how clear your paper is. It will be easy for me to read."
A student volunteers for a difficult assignment.	"That's super."	"I like the way you accept challenges."
A student offers to help explain an assignment to others.	"You're so considerate."	"I like the way you think of others and offer to help them when you have work of your own."

Source: J. Carlson and C. Thorpe, *The Growing Teacher* (Englewood Cliffs, NJ: Prentice Hall, Inc., 1984). Reproduced with permission.

Phrases that focus on helping and strengths include:

- "Thanks, that was a big help."
- "It was thoughtful of you to …"
- "Thanks, I appreciate …, because it makes my job easier."
- "I really need your help on …"
- "You have skill in … Would you share it with the rest of the class?"

Phrases that recognize effort and progress include:

- "I see you're moving along."
- "Wow, look at the progress you've made!" (Be specific and tell how.)
- "You're improving at …" (Be specific.)
- "You may not feel that you've reached your goal, but look how far you've come!"
- "It looks as though you've really thought this through."
- "It looks like you really worked hard on your homework."

The success or failure of encouraging remarks will be a direct function of the teacher's attitudes and purposes for using them.

SUMMARY

The consultant knows procedures that can help teachers change beliefs and develop different approaches to working with students. In addition to individual consultation, we believe working with teachers in both educational (STET) and problem-solving groups ("C" groups) is effective. Teachers can learn the skills of effective teaching and how to incorporate them into the daily teaching process. Every teacher–student relationship benefits from a clear understanding and utilization of encouragement. The consultant stresses a positive encouraging approach.

REVIEW QUESTIONS

1. Describe how teachers blame parents for problems with students.
2. How can consultants eliminate the "useless triangle"?
3. Discuss how groups can affect a lack of experience.
4. List examples of effective and ineffective teacher beliefs.
5. Describe how consultants can help teachers change their faulty beliefs.

6. In what skills do teachers need to be proficient? How does STET teach them? What is the special language of encouragement? Can teachers really use these words?
7. In what ways do praise and encouragement differ?

REFERENCES

Agresta, J. (2004). Professional role perceptions of school social workers, psychologists, and counselors. *Children and Schools, 26*(3), 151–164.

Amatea, E., Daniels, H., Brigman, N., & Vandiver, F. (2004). Strengthening counselor-teacher-family connections: The family-school collaborative consultation project. *Professional School Counseling, 8*(1), 47–56.

Bramlett, R., Murphy, J., Johnson, J., & Wallingsford, L. (2002). Contemporary practices in school psychology: A national survey of roles and referral problems. *Psychology in the schools, 39*(3), 327–338.

Carlson, J., & Thorpe, C. (1984). *The growing teacher: How to become the teacher you've always wanted to be.* Englewood Cliffs, NJ: Prentice Hall.

Dinkmeyer, D., Jr. (1980). *Teacher perceptions of discipline problems.* Unpublished manuscript.

Dinkmeyer, D., McKay, G., & Dinkmeyer, D., Jr. (2000). *Systematic training for effective teaching (STET): Teacher's handbook.* Coral Springs, FL: CMTI Press.

Glasser, W., & Carlson, J. (in press). *Consulting with teachers.* Washington, DC: APA Books.

Goldhaber, D. (2002). The mystery of good teaching. *Education Next, 2*(1), 50–55.

Kruger, L., Struzziero, J., Kaplan, S., Macklem, G., Watts. R., & Weksel, T. (2001). The use of e-mail in consultation: An exploratory study of consultee outcomes. *Journal of Educational and Psychological Consultation, 12*(2), 133–149.

Sanders, W., & Horn, S. (1998). Research findings from the Tennessee valued-added assessment system (TVASS) database: Implications for educational evaluation and research. *Journal of Personnel Evaluation in Education, 12,* 247–256.

6

DEVELOPMENTAL CLASSROOM CONSULTATION

In this chapter, you will learn:

- a definition for developmental guidance
- a rationale for primary prevention
- a comprehensive developmental guidance program
- procedures for training teachers
- how to identify effective resource materials

Are we trying to fit round pegs into square holes, or should we change the holes? Students may need diagnosis, therapy, individual or group counseling, and special classes. The decisions to test, counsel, or refer are part of the school's environment. Often consultants help children to adjust to this structure within the school by modifying the social setting of the school. Consultants are concerned with the total school environment, examining ways to change not only the individual but also the system.

Developmental guidance, the focus of this chapter, coexists with diagnosis, counseling, and therapy. It cooperates with these functions, or preferably helps to reduce their need in the school system. Perhaps our approach to developmental guidance can be characterized by questions and a series of answers.

Why do children go to school? To delight in learning! However naive or simple such an answer may seem, it clearly identifies the purpose of our educational system. It is a realistic goal for our children.

The consultant encourages students to learn and to help them in effectively applying their learning to life. The total learning environment is assessed. What promotes or interferes with the learner's abilities? To reach this goal, the consultant works with the significant adults in the child's life — teachers, parents, and administrators. The teacher and parent influence every child 6 to 8 hours each day. Consultants may have access to only six or eight students each day without the developmental approach. Consultants cannot ignore adults.

A mathematical illustration is appropriate. An elementary school teacher with 22 students in a 5-hour day has 110 "influence hours" per week, 550 influence hours per year, at least 18,150 influence hours with the class. If the teacher refers a single student to a consultant who works with that student for 10 half-hour sessions, 5 hours of influence occur; equivalent to one teacher day. This is 1/165th of the teacher's access to the single student and .000275% of the teacher's influence on the entire class.

The approach we advocate, "developmental" or "primary prevention," is a position shared by others:

> One is hesitant to suggest that any monolithic approach to guidance and counseling is the answer. Yet the time has come for us to emerge as a profession whose major tenets are growth — not problems — whose practice arise from a study of what are normal biological and psychosocial growth patterns. Counseling has little to gain and perhaps even less to contribute if it continues to insist on using the clinical psychology approach and its problem-centered emphasis. (Muro & Miller, 1983, p. 258)

PRIMARY PREVENTION

The term "primary prevention" identifies the approach to working in the schools as described in preceding paragraphs. In this chapter, a comprehensive primary prevention approach for the classroom is presented. Developmental activities are part of a primary prevention program.

It is ineffective for a mental health professional or consultant to wait in an office for problems to walk in the door. Primary prevention is a comprehensive strategy that influences the "normal" and "not normal" school population.

The characteristics of primary prevention include:

- it reduces developmental problems
- it is based in Adlerian or another developmental psychology, not just one or two isolated goals
- it requires the cooperation and involvement of the significant adults (teachers, parents, and administrators) in the child's life

(Dinkmeyer & Dinkmeyer, 1984)

A brief view of the medical profession offers a parallel. Some of the greatest medical breakthroughs of this century have been the development of preventive vaccines. In our lifetime, polio, smallpox, and other crippling childhood diseases have been eliminated or greatly reduced. The medical profession did not wait and treat each polio victim. Instead, elimination or control of the cause of polio was a more effective strategy.

The counseling profession has a parallel belief. Gerler (1976) reviewed more than 200 articles on counselor training and job experience. One-third of the articles favored an increase in primary prevention services. Not a single article advocated a decrease. Training in these services becomes part of the consultant's education. However, Schmidt and Osborne (1981) found that primary prevention procedures are not part of most counselor education training experiences. Advocacy for primary prevention is apparently not supported by actual training experiences.

Ten years after Gerler's review, the profession continued to advocate a preventive and developmental role for the counselor. A review of 10 volumes (10 years) of the journal *Elementary School Guidance & Counseling* by Wilson (1986) documents this attitude.

> The editorial leadership of the major journal in elementary school guidance, *Elementary School Guidance & Counseling* (*ESGC*), also has endorsed a developmental approach. Don Dinkmeyer, who served as editor of *ESGC* for the first 6 1/2 years, is a chief proponent of the developmental guidance movement (e.g., Dinkmeyer, 1966, 1971; Dinkmeyer & Caldwell, 1970; Muro & Dinkmeyer, 1977). Developmental guidance helps people at all age levels learn before crises how to become aware of themselves and others, how to draw more on their personal skills and resources, and how to cope with situations in a responsible way. (Wilson, 1986, p. 212)

Developmental guidance skills often parallel elementary school counselor skills. These skills apply to any consultant at the elementary, junior, or senior high school level.

Although developmental guidance has been advocated for 20 years, the approach is not without its critics. This criticism includes the position that guidance counselors should not function in a developmental capacity. The political and social climate of the schools may not favor this approach; however, a paucity of research documents developmental guidance effectiveness.

The literature does not measure the extent of developmental counseling in the schools, but it does measure attitudes and interests. Wilson's (1986) review of articles in elementary school guidance and counseling published from October 1973 through April 1984 showed 117 developmental (35.2%), 129 remedial (38.9%), and 86 unclassified (25.9%) articles.

> Only about one-tenth (11.1%) of these articles, however, provided evidence of the efficacy of a developmental procedure or activity in terms of statistically significant findings. Moreover, there is some indication that the number of developmentally oriented articles that include such documented evidence may be declining. (Wilson, 1986, p. 213)

The literature on developmental counseling gives us perspective. For the consultant, this history is interesting and almost discouraging. We believe primary prevention and development of positive mental health can be delivered by a counselor or any of the other mental health professionals serving as consultants at the classroom level. The classroom, the site of these primary prevention and developmental experiences, must be examined. This perspective is advocated across the decades, including recent professional writings (Akin-Little, Little, & Delligatti, 2004).

WHAT IS A CLASSROOM?

When children walk into the classroom, creative potential can be lost if conformity is expected. Academic achievement in standardized test scores, while an admirable goal, cannot be the only goal of quality education. In the classroom, consultants have the greatest resources and can make major contributions.

Learning can be improved by enhancing the psychological setting. Value can be enhanced by focusing on the climate in the classroom. The consultant can become involved with the learning climate. As we enter the classroom, we will see 20 or more students.

How can the consultant help the teacher reach every student? A useful procedure is to recognize that they are a group. By using group dynamics, an understanding of the interactions among children and between children and adults, the consultant can help students to learn to cooperate with each other. They can learn to value the unique contributions of each individual to the development of the group.

Teachers also benefit from a group approach. They can begin to see similarities between themselves and other teachers. The consultant helps teachers to strengthen students' self-esteem and their social, emotional, and academic needs. This can be accomplished in an atmosphere characterized by:

1. a mutual respect and trust between teacher and child
2. a focus on mutual goal alignment by teacher and student
3. students feeling that they belong to the group
4. an environment that provides safety for the child
5. an emphasis on self-evaluation in addition to evaluation by others
6. a climate marked by identification, recognition, acceptance, and appreciation of individual difference
7. an emphasis on growth from dependence to independence

The preceding list is representative, not comprehensive. It allows the consultant to identify methods to create effective classroom learning atmospheres. The list reflects psychological principles of individuals in groups (the student's movement in each group setting). A goal of developmental guidance is the understanding of self and others. These goals are succinctly summarized by Dinkmeyer and Dinkmeyer (1982):

> Developing an understanding of self and others is central to the education process. The ability to understand oneself and others is a vital, yet often neglected, part of the elementary-school curriculum.
>
> Children are at once thinking, acting, and feeling beings. Their thoughts and actions always involve feelings. They may like some subjects, be excited about and interested in certain media, dislike doing routine drills, be angry with a certain teacher, or be intensively involved with a project.
>
> The feelings that accompany learning have a significant effect on how well children learn. If they have positive feelings, children tend to participate with a high degree of motivation and involvement and are more likely to derive permanent gains from their efforts. If children's feelings are negative, they are poorly motivated, participate minimally, and are less likely to derive permanent gains. (p. 6)

We have characterized the current situation and the faulty assumptions about children and learning that limit the development of human potential. We also have presented a theory of learning and human behavior. However, a philosophy and a theory of learning and human behavior will be of little value if one fails to systematically organize classroom education.

A central problem in reorganizing schools is recognizing how dehumanized the educational system has become. We can document this dehumanization in many areas. The communication between administrative and supervisor levels and teaching staff is often reduced to formal memos, reports, projects, or objectives.

The tendency to minimize informal contact between administration and staff is illustrated by adversarial contacts between school boards and staff. Board members often think of the staff in terms of statistics, positions, and salaries.

If we value grades, authoritarianism, and content, we want a system different from one that values responsibility, independence, involvement, and an open and positive attitude toward learning. One of the goals of this approach is to provide each child with a teacher who is concerned and interested in facilitating the human potential of every child. As a result of this concern, the teacher seeks to both understand and treat the child as an individual.

The teacher organizes the classroom group to facilitate the development of both the individual and the total group. Anything less than this type of commitment on the part of the teacher results in a dehumanized system. Humaneness has little chance of being developed in a system that is basically dehumanized.

FACTORS THAT BLOCK HUMANENESS

Three basic factors impede human development: lack of goal alignment, inappropriate evaluation, and lack of context.

Mutually determined and aligned goals are desirable. The goals in many school handbooks are often different from teacher plans. Paper objectives bear little resemblance to actual classroom activity. A teacher's goals must be taken into consideration in the planning for educational experiences of children. Each teacher should be treated with mutual respect. As a professional, the teacher studies curriculum, the child, and methods for administering, organizing, testing, and evaluating educational experiences.

This approach is different from the current tendency to make changes in response to educational innovation and fads. The procedure for *appropriate evaluation* of students and the school's success can be an obstacle. It often focuses on cognitive development and functions as if education objectives can be assessed solely through achievement tests. If a student is reading, spelling, and doing arithmetic at a given level, this is one measure of success. But is the student truly an effectively functioning human being? A meaningful measure of educational philosophy, objectives, and teaching methods does not stop at the cognitive sphere.

Education is more than the accumulation of information. This learning occurs within a context that includes:

- the student
- the student's peers
- the teacher
- their beliefs about self and others

Ignoring the emotional context of learning leads to much of the negative classroom experiences we have outlined. This can be illustrated in the common experience of failure in mathematics.

If math (and other subjects) is taught in an atmosphere where mistakes are emphasized, where everyone is literally "on the same page," students dislike the subject. If I am not doing well in arithmetic, what does this imply about myself as a person? What am I feeling about myself?

Our feelings about what we can learn directly influence whether we cognitively grasp the ideas. Everyone has experienced academic failures that influenced affective feelings about their abilities in that subject. For some students, the unpleasant feelings pervade most subjects, and the schooling experience "teaches" one to be a failure.

Failure to appreciate and use the context of learning blocks most consultation efforts. Another aspect of the context of learning is understanding the group.

UNDERSTANDING THE GROUP

Each child is a member of the class or group. The social meaning and context of his or her behavior is important. If the teacher believes student behavior can be controlled by seating charts, verbal directives, and other techniques, the group context in which each child exists is ignored.

There are four principles of group interaction:

1. *Students are social beings.* Each child wants to belong to clubs, form friendships, and be a peer group member. Few want to be left out of groups, unless they are extremely discouraged. Students are members of at least three groups: family, class, and friends. This social interaction is inherent in human behavior,

regardless of titles placed on any group. Everyone needs to belong to groups.

2. *All behavior has social meaning and purpose.* Each student's behavior reflects a search for a unique place in the group. Finding this unique place can be challenging. The social meaning and purpose (the goal) of the behavior, or misbehavior, does not have to make sense to the consultant. For example, Kate is a child who repeatedly talks to her neighbors, yet always stops when her teacher reminds her to be quiet. What could be the purpose of this behavior? Is she trying to get everyone's attention? By using the simple technique of misbehavior goal identification, the teacher can "make sense" of this misbehavior. The goals each student adopts express the beliefs about how they belong in a classroom group. The goals do not have to make sense to the teacher, and the student does not have to be aware of the goal.

3. *Lifestyle is expressed through behavior.* The student's behavior is the means through which the goals of life are presented. If a student is not doing well in one area of work but seems capable of the work, what goal is the student pursuing? If we look to external reasons, we may find some legitimate factors. Nutrition, distractions in family life, or personal conflict may be a contributing factor. It is more helpful to look at the internal reasons; the individually chosen behaviors that express the lifestyle. Often the student is expressing a *choice.* For example, it may be a choice to do well, or do nothing at all, in any area of life, regardless of ability. Faced with challenges in a particular subject, the student may give up. From the student's point of view, it makes sense. It is consistent with the context of beliefs about self. A simple rule applies to all persons: *Look at what a person does, not what they say.* This can be characterized as the "trust only movement."

Consider the following examples of actions and words:

- A teacher expresses interest in your suggestions, says she will use them in the classroom, but reports the next week she wasn't able to find time.
- A friend says, "Let's have lunch soon," but never calls.
- An administrator agrees you need more time for planning, but continues to give assignments that make planning impossible.

In each of the examples above, words and actions are inconsistent. Behaviors are a more useful and accurate indication of the person's intention.

4. *Stimulating social interest is essential.* Social interest is a willingness to cooperate for the common good of the group. If Dana wants to do a classroom chore such as feeding the pet or cleaning the chalkboard, she is expressing social interest. When a student is not willing to cooperate in the classroom (e.g., engages in fighting, defiance, sullen withdrawal, or other disruptive movement), a teacher's frequent response is referral to the counselor, or expulsion from the classroom for varying lengths of time. Such actions only reinforce the student's faulty belief about his or her place in the group.

Students want to belong to the group at any cost, even if that place is in the principal's office. Later in this chapter, ideas for engaging group cooperation and stimulating the social interest of discouraged students are presented.

GROUP DYNAMICS

Group dynamics is concerned with the nature of groups, their development, and relationships among individuals, groups, and institutions. Consultants must operate with awareness of group dynamics. This cannot be incidental; it is central to the consultant's role and function in the school.

The consultant is aware that the individual and the group are inextricably intertwined. The mixture of group and individual personalities should result in the development of a group of persons who are aware of these relationships and move toward a goal that is mutually acceptable. Understanding how to change a group can come from various perspectives. Our perspective includes 10 critical points for achieving change in the school:

1. *Cohesiveness.* Those who are to be changed and those who attempt to influence change must have a strong feeling of belonging to the same group. Through equal participation, a feeling of psychological interdependence must be developed.
2. *Attractiveness.* The more attractive the group is to the members, the greater the potential influence of the group. This suggests that a critical issue is the selection of any group in the educational setting and doing things that enhance the attractiveness of the group. This is most often achieved by ensuring that people who are socially powerful or attractive become members of the group. Attractiveness is also influenced by time and location of meetings and strong support of administration. For most

consultants and teachers, selection of the group or classroom may not be easily achieved. In this case, the question becomes "What can I do to increase the attractiveness of this group?"

3. *Values and attitudes.* In order to achieve change, one must identify that values and attitudes are the basis for attraction to the group. Those which are held in common can be used as forces for change. The group will have less influence on attitudes that are not related to the basis for group membership.

4. *Prestige of a group member.* The greater the prestige of a group member in the eyes of others, the more significant the influence. The implications for the consultant include the assessment of the "prestige" of each group member.

5. *Group norms.* Efforts to change individuals or groups to make them deviate from group norms will encounter resistance. The pressure to conform to group norms must be considered in any strategy to achieve change.

6. *Perception of need for change.* Everyone in the group should share perception of the need for change if the source of pressure for change is to lie within the group. Members must have a clear conception of purpose and personal commitment to individual and group goals.

7. *Communication.* Changing the group requires the opening of communication channels. All persons affected by the change must be informed about the need for change, plans for change, and the consequences of change.

8. *Change and strain.* Changes in one part of a group produce strain in other related parts. This strain can be removed only by eliminating the change or readjusting the parts. Frequently a change in the substructure, such as a pairing of friends or opponents, will create increased tension in the total group.

9. *Goals.* Some of the most significant forces in the group include: goals, aspirations, leadership, anticipations, attitudes, and cohesiveness. In order for a group to become meaningful, a group goal must emerge. Unless the group is working toward some announced goal, it will tend to be unproductive until the goal is clarified.

10. *Aspiration.* Moderate but realistic increases in the level of aspiration tend to generate a comparable increase in performance. Aspirations are essential to a group that wants to succeed, and they tend to result in both individual satisfaction and increased group performance. Therefore, moderately increasing the level of

a group goal will usually result in a corresponding increase in the level of group performance.

THERAPEUTIC FORCES

To discuss therapeutic forces in developmental classrooms may seem strange. These forces help us understand the need for a climate of growth, cooperation, and understanding. They are "therapeutic" in the sense they contribute to the well-being of the classroom. Time spent developing these attributes contributes to the overall benefit of the group.

Table 6.1 presents ten forces important in the development of a healthy group (i.e., classroom, teacher, or parent). The following discussion presents the important aspects of each therapeutic force.

Acceptance

The skill of acceptance and mutual respect is the cornerstone of an effective, helpful classroom. If the teacher or consultant can share the ideas of reflective listening, this is promoting acceptance. We do not think this is appropriate for the younger grades, but at some point (usually much earlier than we initially think), students are capable of listening and responding to others' statements.

If students are too young for this activity, the ability to expand the feeling word vocabulary can be a step in this direction. Students can work on expressing themselves with more than the same old "mad, glad, sad, or bad" feeling words.

Mutual respect can be stimulated by the following specific activities:

1. Students can pick a classmate to know better, through a talk about interests, siblings, or hobbies. Then each student introduces the partner to the rest of the class. If students are too young to introduce each other, the teacher can spend time each week introducing one of the students, focusing on these same areas of interest. Most students enjoy being the center of attention and through this activity develop an appreciation for the similarities and differences between classmates.
2. Discussions where each student shares one personal strength and finds one strength in a classmate.
3. Encouraging empathy among students by simply noticing when they are being sensitive to each other. In addition, modeling of empathy by adults sets the state for these behavior and attitudes in the students.

TABLE 6.1 Therapeutic Forces in Groups

Force	Purpose	Example
Acceptance	To develop mutual respect and empathy among group members.	"I can see you're being sensitive to Joshua's feelings."
Ventilation	To acknowledge and promote the expression of feelings, often by using reflective language.	"You seem very angry about this idea."
Spectator learning	To help students understand their own concerns as they listen to other group members discuss similar concerns.	"How can you apply our discussion of Jim's problem to your brothers and sisters?"
Feedback	To let students know how others perceive their behavior, often by encouraging use of I-messages.	"Could you please tell Carlos how you feel when he teases you?"
Universalization	To help students become aware that they are not alone in their concerns, that most students have similar concerns.	"Who else has wondered about that?"
Reality testing	To help students experiment with new behavior.	"Let's role-play this problem and try out new ways of dealing with it."
Altruism	To encourage students to help each other, rather than compete.	"Beth, I really appreciate your helping Ricky with the math problems."
Interaction	To foster students' social skills and help establish an encouraging classroom atmosphere.	"Meg, share with Joyce how you felt when she said she enjoyed playing with you at recess."
Encouragement	To stimulate students' courage and social interest. To help students become more optimistic about solving problems.	"I think your study habits will help with your project."

(Continued)

TABLE 6.1 Therapeutic Forces in Groups (*Continued*)

Force	Purpose	Example
Cohesiveness	To help students belong to the group.	"We're really working together."

Ventilation

Students express emotions in the classroom, whether we "permit" this to occur or not. In a democratic or effective classroom, students feel free to share their feelings, which can be promoted by:

1. expanding the feeling word vocabulary
2. sharing appropriate feelings through I-messages
3. noting opportunities for students to share unexpressed emotions
4. holding discussions that have, as a focus, the sharing of feelings

During a classroom day, week, or month, many different emotions are experienced. The purpose of acceptance and ventilation is to give these emotions an opportunity to be expressed.

Spectator Learning

Students can learn from each other's similar concerns. The value is in discussing problem situations, because doing so allows that problem to be discussed simultaneously and allows other students with similar concerns to "learn as a spectator." Topics for such learning experiences include, but are not limited to, test anxiety, disappointments about jobs, concerns for the future, handling rejection, learning how to make new friends, and learning how to solve problems.

Feedback

The purpose of feedback is to give students clues as to how they are coming across in the group. Self-awareness can be increased when feedback is used appropriately. Feedback does not blame, accuse, or expect change by the other party. It simply states how the person is being experienced by another person.

For example, a student is constantly interrupting in a small class discussion. Feedback from either the teacher or students would state, "I feel upset when you dominate the discussion, because (I) others can't say what they want." Although change is not expressed in this statement, the foundation for change is laid in the dissatisfaction.

Feedback is a term with which mental health professionals are familiar. It may even be overused or misunderstood. In our context, we see feedback as simply an expression of feeling without criticism, but with the encouragement for change.

Universalization

A good group, or classroom, depends on how well students realize their similarities with each other. Universalization is the process of working with students so they can see these similarities. This can be expressed as follows:

1. Asking, "Has anyone else ever …?" (Referring to a situation likely to be experienced by others.)
2. Asking, "Who else has …?"
3. Discussions of topics that are likely to have broad appeal for students. This is similar to the idea of spectator learning, and topics can be used to promote universalization.

Reality Testing

The opportunity to experiment with new ways to respond to people is known as reality testing. Although the concept sounds abstract, each of us "tests reality" anytime we do something new or different.

One way to make this part of a group is having the group leader model the ability to try new things. In the lower grades, it may be through encouraging small steps and seemingly minor movements. In the upper grades, modeling the "courage to be imperfect" can be a good way to encourage reality testing. Role-play is also an excellent way to test reality.

Altruism

The process of encouraging cooperation, at the expense of competition, is altruism. Although competition is a necessary part of schools, it is overemphasized and has negative effects. Altruism is also known as *finding ways to help each other*. Fostering altruism is a process of creating opportunities for the students to help each other. A process as simple as a "buddy system" is, in a real sense, fostering altruism.

Interaction

Some teachers report they want the interaction to be polite and cooperative at all times. Interaction between themselves and the students, and then between students should all be polite. Encouraging positive interactions between students, such as opportunities to work together without supervision, fosters the opportunity for appropriate interaction.

Encouragement

Although we have left this group force as the last one, it is perhaps the most important. Focusing on strengths and assets, stimulating social interest, and increasing an optimistic attitude are all part of the encouragement process.

Cohesiveness

Cohesiveness plays a significant role in group dynamics. The properties of a cohesive group include change both in the formation and the maintenance of the group. When a group is cohesive, it is in the working stage of development. Movement is toward goals and members feel encouraged.

The ten therapeutic forces in groups can be forces for recognizing and encouraging positive behaviors in the classroom. The peer pressures of the classroom can be understood and used with the proper understanding of these group forces. The usefulness of these forces is summarized as follows:

- The group develops its cohesiveness around guidelines for freedom and responsibility.
- Group members help set goals, make decisions, and institute changes.
- Whenever possible, students proceed at their own level, reducing competition and stressing cooperation.
- Students talk openly and honestly with each other and the teacher and other adults in the school system.
- An atmosphere of mutual respect and trust is developed.
- Encouragement is the prime motivator.

STYLES OF CLASSROOM LEADERSHIP

A useful procedure is for consultants to conceptualize the group leadership role as having three typical expressions: democratic (desirable), autocratic, or permissive (less desirable, but prevalent). Table 6.2 presents characteristics for each of these three approaches to the classroom.

Note the style of leadership directly affects the atmosphere, or climate, of the classroom. Consultants can use this idea to help consultees assess their role in their classrooms. For example, the

TABLE 6.2 Styles of Leadership and Classroom Atmosphere

Democratic	Autocratic	Permissive
Mutual trust; mutual respect.	Control through reward and punishment; attempt to demand respect.	Students may do what they want without concern for others.
Choices offered wherever feasible.	Demands; dominates.	Anarchy.
Motivation through encouragement; identification of the positive.	Focus on weaknesses and mistakes.	All behavior tolerated.
Freedom within limits.	Limits without freedom.	Freedom without limits.
Balance between freedom to work and responsibility to work.	Promotion of dependency or rebellion.	Confusion.
Intrinsic motivation.	Extrinsic motivation and punishment.	Motivation erratic; unpredictable.
Teachers and students set goals together	Activities focus primarily on producing superior products.	Some activities help students make progress and others do not.
Cooperation, shared responsibility.	Competition.	Individual rights without regard for rights of others.
Discipline as educational process; self-discipline encouraged.	Discipline is to establish external control.	No discipline is expected.
Goals are aligned.	Goals are set by teacher.	No positive goals.
Ask for ideas, contributions.	Teacher decides all issues.	No formal decisions reached.

Source: Don Dinkmeyer, Gary D. McKay, and Don Dinkmeyer, Jr., *Systematic Training for Effective Teaching (STET): Teacher's Handbook,* CMTI Press, Inc., © 2000. Reproduced with permission. All rights reserved.

consultee–teacher who is interested in the benefits of feedback but has a permissive atmosphere may find that students misunderstand the idea and use it for "killer" communication, putdowns, or other inappropriate statements.

Leading the Classroom: Group Skills

Classroom management techniques often focus on discipline strategies. They may be nothing more than containment procedures that attempt to stop disturbances or keep them at an acceptable level. If teachers do not understand the purpose of behavior, or have group skills, such techniques will not be successful. It reminds us of the acceptable but ineffective method of popping popcorn — leaving the lid off and standing nearby with a shopping bag!

Consultants must be able to use and teach specific group leadership skills. Teachers can learn these skills in educational groups, practice them in their classroom, and report to and receive support from the group members. Table 6.3 presents 12 group leadership skills. The skills are equally appropriate for consultants when dealing with teacher groups.

Structuring

Structuring is the most important group skill. The leader establishes the guidelines for the discussion or activity, clarifies any misunderstanding, and states the purpose of the meeting.

> **Classroom Example:** "Let's talk about the damage to the bookshelves — we need to do something. Who'd like to start?"

> **Teacher Group Example:** "The purpose of this group is to introduce new ideas you might use in your teaching, to practice these ideas, and to receive support from fellow teachers."

Structuring is often understood as the art of stating the obvious. This is correct! Too often a discussion does not achieve its objectives when those objectives are left unstated. It is the rare meeting, discussion, or class activity that does not benefit from structuring statements.

Universalizing

Universalizing is the process of helping students realize that their concerns are shared. It can be verbalized by the comment, "Who else has felt that way?" when the group leader senses that the topic has been felt or experienced by others. In teacher groups, universalization is a process, not a single comment. It is fostered by the consultant creating opportunities for the teachers to share similar concerns and challenges.

TABLE 6.3 Group Leadership Skills

Skill	Purpose	Example
Structuring	To establish purpose and limits for discussion.	"What's happening in the group now?" "How is this helping us reach our goal?"
Universalizing	To help students realize that their concerns are shared.	"Who else has felt that way?"
Linking	To make verbal connections between what specific students say and feel.	"Bill is very angry when his brother is late. This seems similar to what Joan and Sam feel about their sisters."
Redirecting	To promote involvement of all students in the discussion and to allow teachers to step out of the role of authority figure.	"What do others think about that?" "What do you think about Pete's idea?"
Goal disclosure	To help students become more aware of the purposes of their misbehavior.	"Is it possible you want us to notice you?" "Could it be you want to show us we can't make you?"
Brainstorming	To encourage an atmosphere of shared ideas without evaluation, criticism, or final selection.	"Let's share some of the good things we know about Stanley."
Blocking	To intervene in destructive communication.	"Will you explain your feelings?" "I wonder how Stanley felt when you said that?"
Summarizing	To clarify what has been said and to determine what students have said.	"What did you learn from this discussion?" "What have we decided to do about this situation?"
Task setting and obtaining commitments	To develop a specific commitment for action from students.	"What will you do about this problem?" "What will you do this week?"

(Continued)

TABLE 6.3 Group Leadership Skills (*Continued*)

Skill	Purpose	Example
Promoting feed-back	To help students understand how others perceive them.	"I get angry when you talk so long that the rest of us don't get a turn. What do others think?" "I really like the way you help us get our game started."
Promoting direct interaction	To get students to speak directly to each other when appropriate.	"Would you tell Joan how you feel about what she said?"
Promoting encouragement	To invite students directly and by example to increase each other's self-esteem and self-confidence.	"Thank you for helping us out." "Who has noticed Jamie's improvement?"

Source: Don Dinkmeyer, Gary D. McKay, and Don Dinkmeyer, Jr., *Systematic Training for Effective Teaching (STET): Teacher's Handbook,* CMTI Press, Inc., © 2000. Reproduced with permission. All rights reserved.

Linking

Linking occurs when the consultant points out who has what in common. For example, the statement "It seems like A and B have X in common" is an effort to link A and B on the concept of X. Similar concerns which are often found as "X" concepts in teacher groups can be focused on the ineffective teacher beliefs discussed in an earlier chapter. For example, teachers are often concerned about getting students to cooperate all of the time, to be perfect, or to not make mistakes.

Redirecting

Redirecting occurs when the consultant wants the teachers to talk directly with each other instead of through the consultant as switchboard operator. If a teacher is directing a comment to another teacher, it should be directed to that teacher.

Goal Disclosure

Goal disclosure occurs when the group is working on behavior anecdotes. For each incident, the purpose is to guess the goal of the misbehavior.

Brainstorming

Brainstorming is the process of accepting all ideas when a solution is sought, without evaluating or negating any of the ideas. This can be particularly helpful when considering new strategies.

Blocking

Blocking is the important process of intervening in destructive communication. Consultants do not have to be solely responsible for blocking, but must set the tone through structure, rules, or modeling.

Summarizing

Summarizing can occur at any time, but is particularly helpful when one wants to learn what has happened in the group. This skill provides each member an opportunity to share what has been important for him or her. It also allows the leader to learn what has been important for the members. It can be started by the direction to complete the sentence, "I learned …" Summarizing is an excellent opportunity for everyone to give an equal amount of time to the group.

Task Setting and Obtaining Commitments

Task setting and obtaining commitments relates to the process of making discussions and ideas into concrete, behavioral actions. For example, a student might say, "I want to do better in that subject." This is vague and gives only a general intent. Task setting is the process of deciding what it will take to achieve the "better" in that subject. You also can help the entire class set tasks.

In teacher groups, we have found that teachers (consultees) have a similar tendency to have good intentions but not necessarily the ability to make their intentions specific. In this case, the consultant's task is to make the teacher aware of what will be different, as specifically as possible. General ideas such as "I want to do better" or "My class should be more cooperative with each other" have more specific counterparts, accomplished through task setting and obtaining commitments.

Commitments should be as behavioral as possible and should be for a specific period of time. Be wary of statements such as "I'll never do that again," or "I'll try that idea." Most consultation relationships have opportunities for follow-up; make the commitment for only the period of time between meetings. From this basis, the consultant and consultee can build some momentum toward their goals.

Promoting Feedback

Promoting feedback is the process of exploring how one is perceived by others in the group. It is directly related to the therapeutic force of feedback within groups.

Promoting Direct Interaction

Promoting direct interaction allows students to speak directly with each other. Instead of mediating in disputes, allow students to work out their differences.

Promoting Encouragement

Promoting encouragement is the process of finding what is right or okay in the teachers and letting them know it. It is the ability of the consultant to determine the assets and abilities for each consultee. From that knowledge, encouragement helps the person to consider alternatives.

The process of memorizing these group forces and group leadership skills will not make one a better group leader or teacher. The process of working with groups with an awareness of these forces and skills does make one a better leader.

SUMMARY

Many consultation challenges involve teachers. A helpful procedure is to recognize a set of common and detrimental teacher beliefs concerning their part in the change process. A consultant then must decide how to deal with the teachers, whether as a group or on an individual basis. If the group is used, several group forces can be used and group leadership skills will help to make it a productive problem-solving and educational experience.

REVIEW QUESTIONS

1. What is guidance, and how does the consultant use guidance activities?
2. What does the term "primary prevention" mean? What does it imply for the consultant?
3. What are two principles of groups?
4. What are two therapeutic forces of a group?
5. What are two leadership skills?
6. Why would a consultant choose to use a group for delivery of consultation services?

REFERENCES

Akin-Little, K., Little, S., & Delligatti, N. (2004). A preventive model of school consultation: Incorporating perspectives from positive psychology. *Psychology in the Schools, 41*(1), 155–163.

Dinkmeyer, D., & Dinkmeyer, D., Jr. (1982). *Developing understanding of self and others: DUSO I.* Circle Pines, MN: American Guidance Service.

Dinkmeyer, D., Jr., & Dinkmeyer, D. (1984). School counselors as consultants in primary prevention programs. *Personnel and Guidance Journal, 62,* 464–466.

Dinkmeyer, D., McKay, G., & Dinkmeyer, D., Jr. (2000). *Systematic training for effective teaching (STET): Teacher's handbook.* Coral Springs, FL: CMTI Press.

Gerler, E. R. (1976). New directions for school counseling. *School Counselor, 23,* 247–251.

Muro, J., & Miller, J. (1983). Needed: A new look at developmental guidance and counseling. *Elementary School Guidance and Counseling, 17,* 252–260.

Schmidt, J. J., & Osborne, W. L. (1981). Counseling and consulting: Separate processes or the same? *Personnel and Guidance Journal, 55,* 339–354.

Wilson, N. S. (1986). Developmental versus remedial guidance: An examination of articles in elementary school guidance and counseling, vol. 8–18. *Elementary School Guidance & Counseling, 20,* 208–214.

7

PARENT AND FAMILY CONSULTATION

In this chapter, you will learn:

- why it is important to work with parents
- parent group education strategies
- a problem-solving "C" group for parents
- an approach to family counseling and therapy

Parents and siblings exert the most significant influence on the development of the individual. The family is the arena in which love, trust, acceptance, and a sense of belonging are cultivated. Divorcing the family from the school's setting or the consultant's responsibilities is unrealistic.

In this chapter, you will learn how to work with parents. Educational and therapeutic interventions are presented. We stress the importance of preventive, educational programs and detail how the consultant can establish these programs.

RATIONALE

With few exceptions, the family and, in particular, parents exert the most significant influence on the development of an individual. The child's position in the family constellation and his or her relationship with siblings also exert a tremendous impact. If this structure is unhealthy, a negative and harmful influence results, characterized by fear and atypical growth.

Although the past few decades have seen, in our opinion, a lessening of many positive influences of the family, to ignore the tremendous impact of the family on personality development would be foolish. The influences of the family, both positive and negative, continue to have a profound impact on each individual in our society (Amatea, Daniels, Brigman, & Vandiver, 2004).

Look back on your own personality development to see the connections. The family environment is where the original meanings about life are obtained — the meaning of trust, love, adequacy, and acceptance. From this place within the family, a child perceives beliefs, customs, myths, and values. The family supplies the context for dealing with feelings of superiority and inferiority. In the family is where the individual formulates a view of self as a social, working, sexual, and spiritual being, developing fundamental allegiances with others.

The family becomes the first socializing agency as parents and siblings help the child to develop an identity and to find a place in the world. The basic education of the individual is emotional, and socialization first takes place within the family. The family should never be underrated in terms of its effect upon the learning of the individual. Family of origin has an effect on consultants and their skills. Professional impasses may be due to themes learned in childhood. For example, fear of making mistakes, often emphasized in parent–child relationships, can create struggles for consultants (Haber & Hawley, 2004).

PARENT EDUCATION

Parents seldom have adequate experience, training, and educational background to enable them to function effectively in their role as child caregiver. An employment ad in the classified section of your newspaper might read: "WANTED: Guaranteed employment for 15 to 20 years. Invest $80,000 to $125,000 of your own money, long hours, immense challenges, satisfaction not guaranteed. No prior experience or education required." This imaginary advertisement accurately depicts the nature of the parent's job responsibilities. When you work with parents, you work with the "employees" who have been "hired" for this job. Consultants to parents can focus on their educational opportunities.

In the Adlerian approach to parent education, normal or adequate parents have an opportunity to increase their parenting skills with their children. One need not necessarily be sick, deviant, or troubled to be assisted by a consultant. The attitudes, ideas, and interrelationships of parents are frequent sources of problems. The struggle involved with obtaining independence from their own autocratic background or permissive patterns does not help parents to establish democratic approaches to deal effectively with their children. Often, it produces a backlash; autocratic upbringing leads to permissive parenting. New techniques in democratic management of children are no longer a matter of choice, but of necessity. A healthy family unit is the most important ingredient in a healthy society.

Parent education is an increasingly important task for school mental health consultants. It provides an opportunity, in educational settings, for maximum growth in the family. The attention given to the development of parent education programs has been increasing (Clark, 1995).

Parent education is much different from some of the traditional vehicles for parent involvement schools that have long been emphasized. Organizations such as parent–teacher associations are an example of long-standing parent groups in most school systems. Some significant issues, however, are not being met in this structure.

Parental involvement must be beyond the typical one-time meetings, such as at report card conference time or the evening open house teacher meeting. Any program of consulting, counseling, or remediation that proposes to help an unproductive person must be able to bring about changes in family relationships. Traditionally, the school has not provided assistance in helping families to establish policies and principles related to human behavior (Dinkmeyer & Dinkmeyer, 1976).

The consultant accepts the challenge of restructuring the school by seeing opportunities in the home and community. This role is perhaps best characterized as "an architect of change." Our concern with the whole child recognizes the importance of working with parents. Often there is resistance by parents to the idea of discussing their real problems in the school setting. The consultant deals with this by going to the parents, not only to listen to their problems but also to teach parents skills for solving problems.

A program of parent education that centers on weekly parent group discussions is also an integral component. It allows parents to take an active role. Such groups are formed to help parents understand and work with the affective and cognitive aspects of dealing with their children. Once a program has begun, it becomes self-supporting. Despite common misconceptions, our experience has been that parents, regardless of socioeconomic status, intellectual level, or ethnic background, want, even seek out, and support this activity. Perhaps the effectiveness of parent education can be attributed to the many advantages that participants derive:

- Parents find their concerns are often common to concerns raised by other parents.
- Consultants who do not have children do not have to answer the "How can you understand if you don't have kids?" questions, because within each group are many who are "qualified" in that aspect.
- Groups are opportunities for parents to learn from each other.
- Parent education is a method that provides new ideas, skill practice, and encouragement to place the new ideas and skills into each family.
- The parent education group is cost-effective, reaching not only the 10 to 12 participants, but also their children and spouses. The consultant's sphere of influence while running the group is large, often exceeding two dozen within one group of 10 parents.

Every consultant should be well acquainted with the parent education materials that are currently available and be a competent parent education leader. Consultants who are interested in reaching the greatest number of persons will develop a program to train additional parent education leaders.

Two programs that focus on parent education through book study — Dreikurs and Soltz's (1964) *Children: The Challenge*, and Dinkmeyer and McKay's (1996) *Raising a Responsible Child* — illustrate the concepts discussed in parent education groups. *Children: The Challenge*, by the eminent Adlerian psychiatrist Rudolf Dreikurs and his colleague Vickie Soltz, was perhaps the first significant material used in the parent education field. The book presents Dreikurs's thinking on parent–child relationships and deals with the dilemma in the autocratic/democratic society, it outlines a method of understanding and encouraging children, identifying their mistaken goals, learning how to develop and maintain relationships with teens, winning cooperation, and avoiding undue attention to misbehavior. The numerous, brief chapters are often used in discussion groups.

Raising a Responsible Child (Dinkmeyer & McKay, 1996) is a significant book for individual and group study and is more contemporary in nature. The book deals with the Adlerian approach to understanding human behavior, promoting emotional growth. It gives greater attention to the mistaken concepts of adults and children that interfere with effective parent–child relationships. The book expands the Adlerian approach to include information on communication skills and how to listen more effectively and explore alternatives. Considerable attention is also given to encouragement and logical consequences.

Sections deal with games that children play and explain approaches to problems that children have at school. This book has a guide for effective problem solving when parents are seeking solutions to particular situations.

Although book study groups continue to help many parents, there are inherent limitations to this approach. Book study groups require a high level of skill training by the consultant or group leader. Simply because a book is well written is no assurance of a good group experience.

In addition, these books are written without illustrations, cartoons, clarifying charts, or other aids, which would make them more visually interesting to the parent. These two factors make book study groups available to a smaller portion of the parent population than can be reached through formalized parent education programs. The next step in parent education materials builds on this foundation.

SYSTEMATIC TRAINING FOR EFFECTIVE PARENTING

The Systematic Training for Effective Parenting (STEP) programs are the most widely used Individual Psychology parent education materials (Dinkmeyer, McKay, & Dinkmeyer, 1997, 1998; Dinkmeyer, McKay, Dinkmeyer, Dinkmeyer, & McKay, 1997). STEP programs are focused on three age groups: birth to age six (Early Childhood STEP); six to 12 (STEP); and adolescence (STEP/Teen). As all three programs are philosophically identical, this chapter uses the generic term STEP to refer to all three programs.

The STEP program is organized so that consultants can teach the program with a minimum of experience. Parents who participate in the groups also can become group leaders.

The content of the STEP program focuses on three major concepts:

1. Misbehavior
2. Motivation through encouragement
3. Discipline through choices and consequences

The STEP program is organized as a skill-building program, and it has a systematic instructional sequence. The process usually involves a discussion of a previous week's activity assignment. Parents are asked to do something specific with their children or in observing their children and then report back on the results.

A discussion is held of the assigned reading, focusing mostly on how this reading applies to working with their children. The charts are visual aids for the major concepts and principles of the program and are discussed to reinforce the major concepts.

Parent education groups often consist of approximately 12 members, and they meet once a week for about two hours for seven weeks. Attendance is usually voluntary, although we find increasing use of parent education as part of the judicial system's attempts to remediate abusive and neglectful parents (Dinkmeyer, 1999). Most groups are closed; when a group begins, no new members are allowed to join a group in progress.

While the mix is heterogeneous, the recommendation is that all the parents have at least one child of about the same age so that themes of common challenges particular to an age group can be enhanced. For example, the parents of a teen are often bored by discussions of bedwetting or the challenges of toddlers. Similarly, parents of toddlers are often horrified to learn of the challenges of adolescence to greet them in a decade.

THE LEARNING CYCLE IN PARENT EDUCATION GROUPS

Parent education groups function successfully when the consultant understands areas of leadership skills, the learning cycle, and the stages of the group.

Leadership Skills

1. *Structure the group's time, topics, size, and scope.* Most parent groups meet for approximately 2 hours. Usually 10–14 parents are in each group, and the group meets once each week for seven weeks. The topics of the group should be structured to reflect the educational nature of the group. The group is not therapy.

2. *Seek to universalize the experiences of the group members.* Most parents have had similar challenges raising their children: Bedtime, chores, and motivation are examples of the typical issues. However, parents usually do not recognize that their experiences are similar to those of others in the group. The group leader has the task to of pointing out how their experiences have been similar. Another avenue for universalizing is expectations for their children. Most parents want their children to do well in life, to learn from their mistakes, and to try hard. These goals can be explored, and methods for reaching them are a purpose of the parent education group.

3. *Encourage, encourage, encourage.* You can never be too encouraging with parents in the group. Even when court-ordered,

discouraged parents are in the group, the leader must seek to find what is right or okay about these parents. Simply being in the group is an asset, which can be acknowledged.

The Learning Cycle

1. *New ideas are presented through discussion of the readings and charts.* In most chapters, the ideas presented are new ones, compared to more commonly used ideas. For example, in the chapter on motivation, the new idea of encouragement is contrasted with the idea of praise.
2. *The new ideas are then translated into specific skills.* For example, if the parents understand the idea of encouragement, how do they encourage? What is said or done that is encouraging? Parents practice the skill through role-play, problem situations, and audio- or videotaped incidents.
3. *The importance of using the skills with children is stressed through practical applications.* In most group meetings, the consultant makes certain parents know what their homework for the week will be. This can then be checked and discussed at the start of the next group session.

Stages of the Group

1. *"Great Expectations."* The parents are usually excited and involved, but believe the group will teach them how to "fix" or change their children. Group leaders should spend time structuring the group so that parents understand the goals of the group. Universalizing is also necessary to allow members to begin to recognize the commonality of their concerns. This stage of the group often lasts two or three sessions.
2. *"You mean I have to change?"* Here parents begin to recognize that the parenting group offers ideas to change *themselves*, not the children (although changes in children do result as a consequence of the parents' new behaviors and attitudes). Parents who have no interest in changing their behaviors may become discouraged. This transition stage is an opportunity for the consultant and leader to understand human behavior and encourage any positive movement.
3. *"Cohesiveness and commitment."* The final stage of the group is characterized by cohesiveness and a commitment to change on the part of the members. Many groups find it difficult to end, because the experience has been beneficial for the participants.

Parent involvement in parent education groups goes through predictable stages. This chronology is similar to parent perceptions of many guidance services (Hodgson, Mattison, Phillips, & Pollack, 2001).

THE PARENT "C" GROUP

The "C" group (Appendix II) is a method for helping group members acquire knowledge and evaluate their own beliefs and attitudes. In the "C" group, there is an opportunity to go beyond the study of principles and involves demonstrating not only procedures and ideas, but helping members become more aware of how their beliefs and attitudes affect their relationship with their children (Dinkmeyer & Sperry, 2000).

The power of the "C" group comes from the parent's awareness that a belief such as "I must always be right" or "No one's going to challenge my rules" interferes with effective relationships and caring communication. Parents are helped to see that their beliefs result in resistance and struggle for power. However, if a belief is modified to "I prefer to be right, but I can make mistakes" or "It would be easier if my authority wasn't challenged as part of growing up," then the possibility for conflict resolution is increased.

Leaders of "C" groups prefer to work with parents who have been in study groups or STEP programs, since a common awareness of the fundamentals of human behavior and common ability to use basic parenting skills exists. In the "C" group the leader then integrates this awareness with their feelings, beliefs, and attitudes to apply the principles to very specific situations. Leaders of "C" groups require much more skill in utilizing group dynamics in dealing with problem solving.

The approach was titled "C" group because each of the forces that make it effective begins with the letter C. The specific components include:

1. *Collaboration.* Working together on mutual concerns as equals is a basic requirement.
2. *Consultation* is received and provided by the members.
3. *Clarification* of member's beliefs and feelings is accomplished.
4. *Confrontation* produces more honest and realistic feedback. A norm is established so that each individual sees his or her own purposes, attitudes, and beliefs and develops a willingness to confront other members with their beliefs.
5. *Concern and caring* permeate the relationships.
6. *Confidentiality.* Whatever is discussed within the group stays within the group.

7. *Commitment* requires that each person make a decision to participate fully and become involved in working on his or her own personal concern.
8. *Communication* between all group members.
9. *Change* is the purpose of involvement and each member determines his or her goals for change.
10. *Cohesion* is a sense of group that helps build each participant's family.

THERAPEUTIC FORCES IN PARENT GROUPS

The "C" group provides a unique opportunity for all parents to become more aware of their relationship with their children. They are allowed to experience feedback from other parents in regard to the impact their parenting procedures have upon their children. This opportunity for mutual therapeutic effect is constantly available. They experience a realization that "all parents have problems" and that solutions are available. The opportunity for parents to help each other and to mutually develop new approaches to parent–child relationships is provided. Corrective feedback from peers has a tremendous effect upon the participant.

The consultant who conducts parent groups must be careful not to establish the groups as if its intentions were to provide information and to deal only with cognitive ideas. This is not a lecture, nor is it a discussion, but truly a group experience that necessitates the use of group mechanisms and dynamic processes that are present in any well-organized therapeutic group. A primarily educational group can have therapeutic results.

The consultant realizes the necessity of reassuring and encouraging the parents (even if only through their good intentions to help the child). The consultant should lead, not push or tell. The "C" parent group is much different from the traditional parent meeting. It emphasizes the treatment of parents as "whole people" and as equals. They are not lectured at or told how they should be, but are dealt with in relation to their own concerns right where they are.

Some of the group mechanisms that are particularly pertinent to "C" group work include:

1. Group identification or a communal feeling. The idea that all are concerned about common challenges, as a willingness to help parents live more effectively with their children.
2. The opportunity to recognize the universal nature of child training problems.

3. Opportunities not only to receive help but to give assistance, help, and love to others, including the opportunity to develop cooperation and mutual help, and to give encouragement and support.

4. The opportunity to listen, which not only provides support, but in many instances provides spectator therapy. Someone else's idea may enable parents to start a new approach to transactions with their child.

5. The mechanism for feedback — the individual gains from listening to and observing others.

ADLERIAN FAMILY COUNSELING

The Adlerian approach holds that most parents mean well but have faulty methods of child training. Therefore, the focus is on providing parents with specific principles and not generalities. Adlerian centers such as child guidance centers and family education associations provide parents with the opportunity to observe practical demonstrations. Parents get involved in group discussions on how to apply these principles to a specific family.

All in attendance are provided an opportunity to learn more effective ways of relating to their children. This is accomplished through observation and identification with the family receiving counseling. Many of the normal problems parents have with children are universal and center around meals, sleep, and dressing. Therefore, in this approach, parents are able to understand their own situation when they observe it in another family. Because of their lack of emotional involvement with children in another family, they can be more objective and understanding of what is occurring.

While the Adlerian approach is based on the assumption that parents and children need to develop new family relationships, the emphasis is on providing education and training — not treatment. The focus is on teaching parents more effective techniques and helping adults and children to become aware of the purposes of children's misbehavior.

Sessions for parents begin with an introductory meeting where rationale and procedures are explained, questions are answered, and a voluntary commitment is made. Usually evening meetings that last one-and-a-half hours are scheduled. Once rapport has been established, the interview with selected parents in front of the group is carefully structured.

The volunteer parents may be asked to describe the routine of a typical day, such as the misbehavior of a child and the reactions or actions of the parent. The counselor continually includes other parents in the group in this discussion. Involvement of other parents is usually limited to guesses about what might be "true" about a child, based on their birth order position or shared behavior incident, and then having the parents verify the accuracy of their guesses. The intent is to be helpful and to gain a better understanding of the family dynamics.

Then, the interviewed parents are asked to leave the room, and the children are brought in to clarify hypotheses made about the children's goals. After the children talk, the playroom director may contribute observations about the children in playroom situations and the teacher may describe the children's classroom behavior. The parent group is then asked for action suggestions, and these are discussed and sorted according to significance.

The characteristic elements of the Adlerian approach in a public demonstration are as follows:

1. *The focus of attention is directed toward the parents, as the parents are generally the problem, not the child.* The child responds only in his or her own way to the experience to which he or she is exposed. Especially, younger children do not change easily as long as the parents' attitudes and approach to the child do not change.

2. *All parents participate simultaneously in a procedure that may be called "group therapy."* In these sessions each case is openly discussed in front of other parents. Many parents gain greater insight into their own situation by listening to the discussion of other parents who have similar problems. In this way an influence is exerted beyond the scope of individual treatment; and the whole community, including teachers, is directed toward a better approach to understanding and handling children.

3. *The same therapist works with parent and child.* All problems of children are problems of a discouraged parent–child relationship. The therapist is confronted with the relationship and must approach it from both ends simultaneously. Working with one party alone is almost a handicap. The speed and course of treatment depend upon the receptivity of parent and child alike. It can be evaluation only if the therapist is in close contact with both.

4. *The problems of the child are discussed frankly, regardless of his or her age.* If the child understands the words, this child also can understand the psychological dynamics, which they describe. Contrary to widespread belief, young children show amazing keenness in grasping and accepting psychological explanations. In general, much more time is needed for a parent to understand the psychological dynamics of the problem than the child; the child recognizes them almost immediately.

5. *If other children are in the family, all of them are discussed, not only the "problem child."* These problems are closely related to the behavior of every other member of the family. One has to understand the whole family and the existing interrelationships, the lines of alliance, competition, and antagonism to really understand the concept and behavior of any one member.

6. *The main objective of our work is the change in the relationships between child and parent, and between or among siblings.* Without such a change, altering the child's behavior, lifestyle, approaches to social living, and concepts of self in relation to others is impossible.

Although family counseling demonstrations require a high level of skill on the part of the consultant, an interesting point to note is the similarities in steps in the processes of both. The "C" group model provided a pattern for parent education, and the concepts are also used in family therapy. A consultant in a school setting would do well to consider the advantages of the family counseling demonstration center as a part of a complete set of services for the community.

STRATEGIES FOR REDUCING PARENT RESISTANCE

Parents can frequently resist any effort at consultation. Resistance can be defined as denying the existence of a problem or as an emotional reaction to a situation. In both cases, there is little movement from a parent in the consultative relationship.

The reasons for resistance are multiple and can include:

1. Prior negative experiences with schools, including a parent's own educational experiences.
2. Personal problems that overshadow the issues relating to the child's problems.
3. Philosophical differences such as "it's the school's problem, not mine."
4. Denial of the very existence of a problem.

(Campbell, 1993)

Potential solutions to this gauntlet of resistance can be seen in a threefold approach:

1. Begin by listening to the presenting point-of-view of the parent. Every story can be reframed.
2. Reframe issues in terms of the strengths present or strengths created through education.
3. Make realistic, practical steps and summarize each mutually agreed commitment.

(Dinkmeyer, 1999)

FAMILY THERAPY

In this section the concepts for Adlerian family therapy are outlined. The terms "therapist" and "consultant" are used interchangeably. While not all consultants would perceive themselves as therapists, understanding the principles behind effective family interventions is helpful. This section may serve as a frame of reference for evaluation referrals to other community professionals. In this section, we outline a strategy that seeks to change the family system using the most direct and economical techniques.

Understanding the Model

Adlerian family therapy is a specific intervention strategy. One benefit of this approach is the large number of concrete procedures for understanding the family. Patterns, goals, and movements within the family are all viewed as possible routes for understanding and improving the family. The consultant, counselor, or therapist is seen as the leader in the relationship. This means he or she would formulate questions and give suggestions that first identify and then reframe the family system.

The concrete procedures and techniques that help to change the family system include extensive use of consultation and parent education. The goal of this model is to change the system (or group) the family has created and to help each individual function within that new system.

History and Development

The tradition of family counseling is strong within Individual Psychology. Alfred Adler quickly established clinics for the purpose of couple and family counseling in Vienna in 1922; and eventually more than 30 were created. One of the most interesting aspects of these centers was the emphasis upon public demonstration. Adler's work is the predecessor to the public family counseling described in this chapter.

Adler and others would counsel or advise a family in a public forum, not in private. This was in stark contrast to other approaches to working with families. In the counseling demonstrations, the therapist might work with members of the family as subsets; for example, beginning with the parents, then all of the children at once, followed by the parents again, and then the entire family. If this was therapy, the family might be seen as a whole for the entire session.

The purpose of the Adlerian approach is threefold: to help the family, to demonstrate to other professionals how to work with families, and to help others understand that their concerns are similar to those being raised by the demonstration family. These demonstrations were the precursor to modern family education demonstrations and modern Individual Psychology counseling and therapy.

Adler continued his work with public demonstrations for several years. His efforts were cut short by the chaotic events preceding World War II. Adler and others were forced to leave Europe and continue their work in other areas, such as North America and Scotland. The influence of Adler's work cannot be minimized. A widely used textbook puts Individual Psychology in this perspective:

> Adler anticipated the future direction of the helping professions by calling upon therapists to become social activists by addressing the prevention and remediation of social conditions that were contrary to social interest and resulted in human problems. Adler's pioneering efforts on prevention services in general health lead him to increasingly advocate for the role of Individual Psychology in schools and families. Because Individual Psychology is based on a growth model, not a medical model, it is applicable to such varied spheres of life as child guidance, parent-child counseling, marital counseling, family therapy, group counseling, individual counseling with children, adolescents, and adults, cultural conflicts, correctional and rehabilitation counseling, and mental health institutions. Adlerian principles have been widely applied to substance abuse programs, social programs to combat poverty and crime, problems of the aged, school systems, business and religion. (Corey, 2005, p. 111)

Corey continued by listing contributions of Adlerian theory to the existential, person-centered, Transactional Analysis, Behavioral, Rational-Emotive, and Reality therapies. Rudolf Dreikurs, a student of Adler, came to Chicago in 1937. He established a Child Guidance Center at Abraham Lincoln Center and other centers across the Chicago area. Dreikurs trained counselors in many other parts of the world, encouraging the creation of Family Education Centers (FECs). Centers were created in more than 20 cities throughout the United States, Canada, and many other countries.

Many of these FECs continue to operate, and new FECs have been established since Dreikurs's death. In many communities, the FEC is a referral source for Adlerian family therapy. Dreikurs had a profound commitment to making Adlerian psychology available to the public. While in Chicago, he founded the North American Society of Adlerian Psychology (NASAP) and the Alfred Adler Institute of Chicago (now Adler School of Professional Psychology), institutions that continue to promote Individual Psychology throughout North America (Dinkmeyer & Sperry, 2000).

Dreikurs made a significant impact on the way we ourselves have worked with families, whether in therapeutic or educational settings. His work on the four goals of misbehavior is a simple yet elegant example of his profound insight into the nature of children's behavior. When complimented about this concept as a "brilliant invention," he is reputed to have replied, "I did not invent them, I simply saw them!" Such was the power and influence of Dreikurs's work.

MAJOR THEORETICAL CONCEPTS

A useful procedure is to see each family member with the following characteristics: he or she is indivisible, social, creative, has decision-making ability, and has goal-directed beliefs and behaviors. This view is holistic. It looks for patterns, unity, and consistency.

All behavior has social meaning. The social context of behavior has been discussed in prior chapters, but it also applies to the family and the relationships within that system. A child's poor schoolwork makes sense when another sibling's excellence in school discourages this child. Father's refusal to do any housework affects not only mother, but all children who see noncooperation as an acceptable male value.

Another concept essential to understanding social context is socially useful behavior or social interest. Examples of socially interested behavior in a family include cooperation, completing assigned or volunteered tasks, and looking out for the welfare of others. While many immediately understand this as the responsibility of the adults in the family, it also is an opportunity for the children and teens of the family to move toward responsible behaviors.

The concept of social interest has profound opportunities for the therapist or consultant. If the family is not cooperating or is dysfunctional, an area for homework or education may be one in which social interest is stressed. Thus, social interest will also be a barometer of the relative health or progress of the therapeutic or educational intervention. In short, if they are getting better, are they doing things for each other?

All behavior has a purpose. As previously stated, all behavior has a goal. The movement toward a goal is revealed in a person's behaviors. Goal-directed behavior in the family is explained by Sherman and Dinkmeyer (1987): "The family therapist can become aware of goals by examining her feelings or by having the members involved in the transactions examine their actions and reactions" (p. 122). For example, in a parent–child conflict, the parent feels annoyed and devotes much time to the child. It may be that the child is attempting to seek the parent's attention. However, if the parent feels challenged and would like to prove that the child cannot do that, it is likely that a power struggle will ensue. And if the parent feels hurt, the child's desire to get even will be apparent. Feeling utter frustration or the need to rescue, the parent will know that although the child is capable, he or she is displaying inadequacy in order to cause the parent to give in and do something for him or her.

Striving for significance. We seek to belong in a significant way, in a way that moves us from a perceived minus to a perceived plus. As children, especially in the first years, we are "less than" by virtue of our age and corollary physical, intellectual, and emotional abilities. The efforts of young children to belong in the family can be assisted if parents and therapist can find ways for these children to contribute, significantly, in positive ways. The opposite of this would be the youngest child who constantly gets his or her way by whining or demanding. He or she is a "significant" disruption in the family, and his or her striving for belonging is seen as a mistaken assumption.

Subjective perceptions. The point of view of each family member is a fertile ground for the therapist:

> It is essential that the therapist understand the perception of the family members. Each person develops and is responsible for his or her subjective view of life. People give all of their experiences meaning. This process has been described as follows: Each person writes the script, produces, directs, and acts out all the roles. We are creative beings deciding our perceptions, not merely reacting. We actually often elicit responses, which help us to maintain our self-perceptions, including negative ones. (Sherman & Dinkmeyer, 1987, p. 123)

THE ADLERIAN FAMILY SYSTEM

Adlerian family therapy is an interactional, or systemic, treatment model. It is not an individual approach that has been adapted to family therapy. What happens between family members is crucial to the Adlerian therapist. The basic principles focus on the social meaning of behavior, purposive behavior, and the movement between and among individuals.

Understanding the family means working with the family as a group. Family interactions are guided by the family's goals, lifestyles, and the private logic of each member as well as the group goal, lifestyle, private logic, and family atmosphere.

Dinkmeyer and Dinkmeyer (1991) suggested that the family interacts around eight dynamic qualities:

- Power and decision making
- Boundaries and intimacy
- Coalitions
- Roles
- Rules
- Similarities
- Complements and differences myths
- Patterns and styles of communication

GOALS OF THE THERAPEUTIC PROCESS

The role of therapist is not often perceived as one that fits a school consultant. However, recent events in our culture have made it more important that school personnel understand the basic methods of successful interaction with the family system.

To that end, we present a series of questions that can help the school consultant shape a role in the intervention or referral for the family. The following questions were first introduced in Dinkmeyer and Dinkmeyer (1991) and have been modified to portray probable issues in a school setting:

1. What does each person want to have happen in the family? Can any of this be achieved by school personnel?
2. What does each family member see as the main challenge or issue faced by the family?
3. Are family members aware that the purpose of these sessions is to focus on change, not merely to complain?
4. Do they understand the nature and duration of the contact with the school consultant?

5. Identify where the family stands on developing family cohesiveness, cooperation, community, and satisfaction. This can be accomplished through questions such as the following:
   a. What is the level of self-esteem? Does each family member have a sense of worth? Does each feel valuable, capable, loved, and accepted?
   b. What is the level of social interest? Does each family member have a sense of belonging, a feeling that they are part of the group? What is the commitment to cooperation, involvement, and sharing?
   c. What is the sense of humor that exists in the family? Can family members see themselves in perspective? Can they make jokes about themselves, accept their mistakes, and have the courage to be imperfect, avoid nagging, supervision, and defensiveness?
6. What roles do various members play in the family? Are they functioning in a variety of tasks, or does each family member have certain restricted roles to play in the family?
7. Who is for or resistant to change? It is important to understand who is seeking change. Are they willing to change themselves? What is the type of change they want in the family, in individuals, and in themselves? Equally important is to analyze and identify who is resistant to change. Clarify the purpose of the resistance and what the person gets for that resistance.
8. The traditional approach is to become involved in the diagnosis of family faults, weaknesses, and psychopathology. Even more important is the diagnosis of the assets of the family. What are the general assets of the family as a unit? What are the assets of each family member? How do they blend into the family system? What resources are available in the extended family and community?

FAMILY CHANGE

Change in the family can include:

- The potential redirection of power
- New understanding and insight
- New or refined goals
- New skill knowledge or options, particularly in communication, problem solving, and conflict resolution
- Increased courage and optimism; a sense of empowerment

- Increased social interest
- New roles within the family system
- Commitment to growth and change

(Sherman & Dinkmeyer, 1987)

Most of the changes can occur in successful therapy, successful counseling, or successful education. A basic principle of the Adlerian approach is to involve the family at the least expensive, least intrusive level appropriate to its needs. This requires clinical or professional judgment on the part of school personnel.

SUMMARY

In this chapter we have presented a comprehensive approach to working with parents. This approach includes parent education, family counseling, and family therapy. The consultant serves as a resource for creating parent education programs. If qualified, the consultant can also conduct family counseling. The consultant needs to understand the concepts of family therapy. Within these concepts lies an understanding of the role of Adlerian psychology for all family members.

REVIEW QUESTIONS

1. What is the rationale for consultation with parents and families?
2. Name two approaches to working with parents.
3. What is the "three-step" cycle of parent education, and what does it imply for the consultant's intervention?
4. What are therapeutic forces in parent groups?
5. How can a "C" group be used with parents?

REFERENCES

Amatea, E., Daniels, H., Brigman, N., & Vandiver, F. (2004). Strengthening counselor-teacher-family connections: The family-school collaborative consultation project. *Professional School Counseling, 8*(1), 47–56.

Campbell, C. (1993). Strategies for reducing parent resistance to consultation in the schools. *Elementary School Guidance and Counseling, 28*(2), 83–92.

Clark, A. (1995). Rationalization and the role of the school counselor. *School Counselor, 42*(4), 283–292.

Corey, G. (2005). *Theory and practice of counseling and psychotherapy* (7th ed.). Monterey, CA: Brooks/Cole.

Dinkmeyer, D., Jr. (1999). Working with court-ordered and mandated parents. *Journal of Individual Psychology, 551*(1), 121–123.

Dinkmeyer, D., & Dinkmeyer, D., Jr. (1976). Systematic parent education in the schools. *Focus on Guidance, 8*(10), 1–12.

Dinkmeyer, D., Jr., & Dinkmeyer, D. (1991). Adlerian family counseling and therapy. In A. Horne (Ed.), *Family counseling and therapy* (pp. 383–401). Itasca, IL: Peacock.

Dinkmeyer, D., & McKay, G. (1996). *Raising a responsible child.* New York: Simon & Schuster.

Dinkmeyer, D., McKay, G., & Dinkmeyer, D., Jr. (1997). *Systematic training for effective parenting.* Circle Pines, MN: American Guidance Service.

Dinkmeyer, D., McKay, G., & Dinkmeyer, D., Jr. (1998). *Systematic training for effective parenting of teens.* Circle Pines, MN: American Guidance Service.

Dinkmeyer, D., McKay, G., Dinkmeyer, J., Dinkmeyer, D., Jr., & McKay, J. (1997). *Early childhood STEP.* Circle Pines, MN: American Guidance Service.

Dinkmeyer, D., Jr., & Sperry, L. (2000). *Counseling and psychotherapy: An integrated, individual psychology approach.* Columbus, OH: Merrill.

Dreikurs, R., & Soltz, V. (1964). *Children: The challenge.* New York: Hawthorn.

Haber, R., & Hawley, L. (2004). Family of origin as a supervisory consultative resource. *Family Process, 43*(3), 373–381.

Hodgson, J., Mattison, S., Phillips, E., & Pollack, G. (2001). Consulting parents to improve a child guidance service. *Educational Psychology in Practice, 17*(3), 263–272.

Sherman, R., & Dinkmeyer, D. (1987). *Systems of family therapy: An Adlerian integration.* New York: Brunner/Mazel.

8

CONSULTATION CASE EXAMPLES

In this chapter, examples of consultation with teachers and parents are presented. The examples have a consistent format, including:

- the age and grade of the student
- the misbehavior or concern
- analysis of the goal or purpose of the behavior
- possible teacher alternatives
- author's comment on the example

In addition, a brief synopsis of the five consultation sessions on the DVD are presented. The DVD has one parent group, two teacher, and two parent consultations. One of the teacher consultations is transcribed in Appendix I.

The reader is urged to consider how the concepts discussed in the book are applied to each example. A systematic sequence of anecdote, diagnosis, and alternatives is presented. The incidents are shared from the teacher's point of view in his or her own words. While each example does not end with a specific resolution, the examples illustrate the methods of consultation, which provide the consultant with a dynamic framework in which to continue the consulting relationship.

The examples do, however, allow the reader to see possible new behaviors for the teacher. A simple technique — DID (do it differently) — is a guiding rule in all consultations. We seek to create alternatives.

The cases illustrate a dynamic use of the psychology outlined in the previous seven chapters.

ELEMENTARY LEVEL
Case 1: Toyonna

Age and setting: Toyonna is an 8-year-old child in third grade.

Behavior: Toyonna likes to tattle on everybody. She can find the smallest thing to tell me every day. Toyonna consumes most of my day with trying to get other students in trouble. It is also my conclusion that she creates situations to get others in trouble. This is an example of one of those situations. Toyonna and Tasha do not get along and they have been told to always stay apart from each other. We were having reading class. Toyonna and Tasha are both in my team teacher's group. They were in her classroom and I was in mine. The other teacher went to use the rest room and I kept an eye on both classes. Toyonna informed me three times that Tasha was following her around the room. This was all in a matter of 5 minutes. I asked some other students if Tasha was following her and they said that Toyonna was following Tasha. Toyonna created the situation and then tattled on Tasha. The last time it happened, Toyonna actually attacked Tasha verbally. She then proceeded to argue with me about the situation. I brought Toyonna into my room and made her sit and read by my desk.

Analysis: Toyonna's behavior goal is attention. Three times she wanted me to stop what I was doing to solve her "problem." She wanted me to notice her and tend to her every whim. I began to feel very annoyed and frustrated with the situation. I gave her warnings and reminded her to stay away from Tasha, but she kept repeating the same behavior. I decided the problem is solvable. I own the problem because my right of having a peaceful classroom is being infringed upon. My lesson was also interrupted three times. Tasha's rights were also interfered with by Toyonna making up her stories. When the problem is fixed, Toyonna will stop tattling and I will be able to teach without unnecessary distraction.

Alternatives

- *Exploring alternatives*: Toyonna and I could explore different ways to deal with problems without tattling. I might brainstorm alternatives, new ways to behave in this situation, with her. Toyonna and I will decide which times are appropriate to come to the teacher and which are inappropriate. We can decide the difference between "good" tattles and "bad" tattles. I might also do this with the whole class to prevent future incidences of this behavior.

- *Make an action plan*: I have decided to use this with Toyonna and it has been very successful. Toyonna and I worked out a plan to reduce "bad" tattling. Her mother bought her a small notebook and some stickers. Each day she writes the date on a new page. Her mother has been very helpful by writing encouraging words on the pages each morning. She tells her how wonderful she is and to have a good day. Toyonna shares these with me every morning. If Toyonna gets through the morning without a "bad" tattle she gets a sticker. She does the same for the afternoon. Toyonna looks forward to this because she gets to choose her own stickers. For the past three weeks she has received two stickers a day at least three times a week. This is a huge improvement and I am very satisfied.

- *Give "I" messages*: If Toyonna knew exactly how I felt about tattling, she may be able to control it. I might give positive "I" messages like, "When you get along with others, I feel happy because cooperation is important." When she tells a "bad" tattle I might say, "I feel frustrated when you tattle." Toyonna has a wonderful sense of humor and she likes to smile and laugh. I might work on tone of voice as well as any humorous nonverbal cues that could indicate I know what is going on. She enjoys participating during lessons and has many good ideas during activities. She can be a caring friend and a loving student. She is also helpful to some of the younger students in the class. I will continue to use the sticker book because she likes it and considers the stickers to be good rewards and positive reinforcement. I will focus on her positive assets and remind her of them. I will be consistent with the action plan and using "I" messages. I believe I can do this because I am focused, patient, and determined.

Comment: This example shows a mild misbehavior pattern in an elementary school student. The teacher correctly identifies the goal of her behavior as attention and has generated a wide variety of alternatives. She reports some success with some of these behaviors. The use of positive reinforcement through sticker books is a traditional teacher tool, and it is blended with the use of the newer idea of positive reinforcement through "I" messages.

Case 2: Larry

Age and setting: Larry is a 7-year-old second grader. He was born addicted to crack cocaine and physically abused until the age of 4. He is currently in a foster home with a single parent. The individual has six other foster children as well. The older children range from the ages of 11 to 19 years old. In the two years he has been with this particular foster parent, he has been expelled from three elementary schools. All of the expulsions are due to his extremely disruptive behavior. When his foster mother used physical punishment (spanking) for Larry, he called 911. This led to Larry being removed from the home for three months. Now he threatens to report anyone that attempts to discipline.

Behavior: Larry enters the classroom mumbling that he hates to come to my room for math. He slams his books down and remains standing. I will say, "Larry, please get your math notebook and begin the problem of the day." Larry will say he does not want to do this stupid stuff. I will give him two to three minutes to begin the assignment. During this span of three minutes, Larry may begin to insult other students. I then give Larry his first warning. The behavior will cease while he works at this seat. Once Larry comes to the carpet to hear the new concept for the center activity, he begins to yell out answers or other irrelevant information. Larry begins to roll around on the floor or make fun of other students who do not understand the concept. After the third warning, Larry is physically removed from the classroom. This is frustrating and at times I get angry inside because of this behavior.

Analysis: Power. I have a tendency to become angry with Larry's behavior and have a disrespectful attitude toward students. When he is in one of his disruptive moods, I think he behaves this way to provoke me into using the "Last Word Syndrome." Larry is only 7 years old and at times it seems impossible that he has such extreme behavior at such an early age. Larry also has a personal assistant, similar to a teacher's aide. The job of the assistant is to teach Larry but to physically remove him from a classroom when necessary. Larry's behavior is recorded by the assistant in 15-minute intervals to determine his reward for the day. This monitoring and rewarding system is becoming less successful.

Alternatives   The following ideas were generated in the consultation:

- *Remove the audience*: Larry baits teachers by attempting to embarrass them in front of other students (revenge). Once the teacher responds, he begins his bid for power.

- *Acknowledge power*: He likes to tell me that I cannot make him do anything. I think if I agree with him, he will be caught off guard. "You're right, I can't make you complete this assignment, but if you don't, you will finish it during your PE or recess time."
- *Written record*: This will let Larry know I plan to remember his exact behavior and share it with the discipline team.
- *Ask a favor*: Larry likes to feel needed and I think this might help his self-esteem.
- *Completely withdraw from the conflict, totally ignoring Larry*: Focus immediately on the other students. This would be similar to the "remove the audience" technique.
- *Make a written record*: The teacher can get out a sheet of paper and tell Larry that she is going to write down everything that he is refusing to do and everything that he is saying.

Some of the alternatives can be structured as encouragement techniques:

- Positive side of student: very bright and friendly.
- Positives of the behavior: Wants to please and be needed in order to express his feelings.
- Positives of the student–teacher relationship: Larry knows I love him and I think he can accomplish all of his goals.

Comment: This is an interesting example of extremes. The student has extreme environment and family problems. He acts out and challenges all adults. At the same time, the teacher sees a large number of practical possible alternatives and includes a subset of specific encouragement techniques. The use of the personal assistant is not discussed, but is also a possible area for a productive consultation.

Case 3: Katie

Age and setting: Katie is a 7-year-old second-grade student who is in my classroom for the majority of the day.

Behavior: During a science lesson, Katie talked and laughed with other students at her table. Although other students responded to "the eye" and name-dropping, Katie did not. She would stop her behavior only temporarily and avoided eye contact with me. I felt extremely annoyed with her, then I became angry. No matter what I did with her or with other students around her, she would temporarily stop the behavior but resume it sooner or later.

Analysis: The goal of the misbehavior began as attention-getting. As the behavior continued it became more of a power struggle.

Alternatives

- *Stand close by*: I might try standing closer to Katie during instruction. I like conducting large group instruction with most students seated on the carpet: however, Katie usually manages to be near the back of the group. I could give her an assigned spot on the carpet in closer proximity to me.
- *Give written notices*: Dropping a note on her desk during instruction reminding her to not disturb others, or writing her a longer note after class telling her of my concerns about her behavior, might help solve the problem in a discreet manner.
- *Use a "to you ... to me" message*: A verbal message stating, "To you science class may not seem important, but to me it is important that all my students have a chance to learn and be successful in science," may help express my need for Katie to be more attentive and to stop distracting others.
- *Have a conference*: I could have a conference with Katie to discuss her behavior. She could help brainstorm ways to improve her attention during science. At this time, we could set some logical consequences. For example, if she does not get the science notes copied during science time due to talking, she would have to stay in at recess to complete the assignment. The next time the misbehavior occurs, I am going to give Katie the choice between not talking to others and moving beside me on the carpet. If this does not help, I'm going to use a "To you ... to me" message, and last of all I will write her a note and set up a conference to discuss her behavior. My strength that will increase the likelihood of following through with this plan is my confidence in Katie: that she wants positive attention, but is seeking it in inappropriate ways. I will also follow through because I am consistent in the classroom and feel it is very important for students to pay attention. Finally, I will follow through because I know the techniques I have tried before have not fixed the problem. It is important to my instruction and Katie's self-esteem that this problem gets resolved in a respectful manner.

Comments: The teacher has created a large number of new behaviors. The teacher also sees personal (teacher) strengths that can contribute to the change in the behavior pattern with Katie.

Case 4: Alissa

Age and setting: Alissa is a 6-year-old kindergartener in the afternoon group.

Behavior: When afternoon kindergarten students arrive at school, they are to sit at the cafeteria table. No one is to approach the teacher until all morning students are dismissed. Every day, Alissa breaks this rule and approaches the teacher with some type of attention-getting behavior. Specifically, one time she came to me and said, "When do we get to go to class?" I said, "You know the rule, please sit down." She stopped for a moment but then, at her table, began a temper tantrum. This lasted for 5 to 10 minutes. I ignored her, but when we had to move to the classroom, I picked her up. The screaming continued and when we got to the classroom, she grabbed my leg and would not let go.

Analysis: This begins as an attention-getting ploy but quickly turns into an intense power struggle. I do not usually give in. However, there are circumstances that I think contribute to this situation, at least I am aware of them whenever I consider new alternatives in the daily situation.

Alternatives   Before choosing the intervention techniques, I considered the child's background and home life. Alissa comes from a very abusive home. She was taken from her mother and is allowed no contact. Although she is in the custody of her father, she lives with her grandmother. When Alissa does stay with her father, his other three children are present. These children do not have the same mother as Alissa.

The courts have stated that no parent or guardian is to use any type of physical punishment (spanking). During her controlling behavior, she reminds her teacher, "You or no one else can do anything to me." It is unfortunate that she thinks nothing can be done, but I am attempting to see things I can do differently

- *Completely withdraw from the conflict and focus on the other students*: I will refuse to take the hook when Alissa is baiting me for a power struggle.
- *Remove the audience*: I will ask Alissa to leave my room and return when she can behave in the appropriate, expected manner that the other students are modeling.
- *Make a written record*: I will make a written record of any incident in which Alissa refuses to cooperate with the teacher. I will make a copy of this record to send home for her father and her grandmother to see.

- *I will acknowledge the student's power*: I will agree with Alissa that, "You are right, I can't make you finish your paper, but if you don't, you will complete it during free time."
- *The teacher will take charge of her negative emotions*: I will work to keep my negative emotions from being seen both verbally and nonverbally.

The positive side of Alissa is that she does not lie. She will admit whenever she hits or kicks someone, and she will tell her father and grandmother about every incident that occurred during the school day (even admitting that she hit someone for no reason). Alissa is also a very loving child. She wants to be liked by all of the other students and she runs to me for a hug countless times each day. She does trust my judgment and accepts any consequences that she receives. The positive side to her goal of power is that she is a very determined little girl and loves to interact with others.

Comment: The case of Alissa could be "explained away" by her family life. The teacher considers these influences but moves to what can be done in the school setting. It is interesting to note the assets seen in Alissa, and the creation of a perceptual alternative; the student's power struggle is seen as being very determined.

MIDDLE/JUNIOR HIGH LEVEL
Case 5: Joe

Age and setting: Joe is a 14-year-old eighth-grade student.

Behavior: Joe has been diagnosed with emotional behavior disorder (EBD). Joe enrolled at our middle school after fall break. My initial reaction to Joe was very positive because he seemed to have a good attitude and manners. However, it did not take long for Joe to create some misbehaviors. Within the first month of attending our school, he was suspended for fighting, cussing, and threatening teachers.

Because I am the assistant principal, I do not have direct contact with this student. I can relay incidents as I understand them. He had been removed from two previous schools and his father and step-mother have just transferred into our district. When I attempted to frame this as a "last chance" for Joe, he shrugged his shoulders and gave me a look that said "I've heard this before, and I don't care."

Our EBD teachers who work with Joe said that he seemed to be discouraged but was not very passive in his discouragement. He makes many situations into power struggles. Joe always had to demonstrate that he was in control, and if things did not go his way he was going to find ways to make everyone miserable. For example, Joe would refuse to do homework assigned to him and said that nobody could force him to do it. Nevertheless, we were not going to give up because we realized that he needed people to care for him, and we saw that he had some strong characteristics to work with that would enable him to be successful in our classroom setting.

At the same time, staff reports he can be reached through specific appeals for help or assistance. For example, he was willing to hand out worksheets to all students. He is willing to discuss sports, and prides himself in being very knowledgeable about specific teams and players.

Analysis: Joe purses power both actively and passively.

Alternatives

- *Provide choices:* He can either do the assignment given to him or experience the previously stated consequences for his misbehavior.
- *Provide natural and logical consequences:* If Joe chooses not to sit down to do his assignment, then he will have to either stand up and do it or sit by the principal's office to complete the assignment. Basically, he is once again provided with a set of choices.
- *"Exploring alternatives" such as role reversal and offering tentative questions:* I try to trade places with Joe and ask him what he would do if he were the teacher and he had a student who refused to do his assignments. It surprised me when he responded by saying that he would always expect his students to complete their assignments without question.

Comment: Joe is a discouraged student displaying "power" as his goal of misbehavior. These recommendations are efforts to treat him fairly and encourage him to learn from his choices. This is an excellent example of moving past a student file with a long history of failures and act "as if" good things will come from a student. The teacher's reported success with the third idea (exploring alternatives through role reversal) is an excellent example of taking a risk by doing something different in the teacher-student relationship.

HIGH SCHOOL LEVEL
Case 6: Juan

Age and setting: Juan is a 16-year-old junior in high school.

Behavior: Juan is a student in my junior U.S. history class this semester. Juan is surrounded by football players, cheerleaders, and those that the students in the class one day defined as "rednecks" to the exchange student who is also in the class. Everyone is vying for attention. The football players will do or say just about anything to get a laugh from the class and a smile from the cheerleaders, and those "rednecks" love to rile up the rest of the class with their off-the-wall comments and rude "What I did over the weekend" stories. And then there is Juan.

Juan is a good student, but he attracts my attentions in a different way. He constantly interrupts me during class to ask me to repeat things that I have already repeated twice. There was one particular day that Juan was particularly active. It was to the point that he was not only getting my attention, but everyone else's in the room also. By the fourth or fifth time that he interrupted me, the other students were beginning to roll their eyes, sigh loudly, and make comments to their neighbors. A student nearby even offered Juan her paper so that he could just copy her notes. I know that this behavior is not because he does not understand; he participates in class day in and day out and has one of the highest grades in the class. I was very annoyed.

Analysis: The goal of Juan's behavior is attention. This is evident by looking at the way that it made me feel — annoyed. Juan is preventing me from teaching.

Alternatives I have several options to solve this problem. I could ignore Juan when he is wanting attention in this manner. I could stop the first time that this behavior happens and tell Juan that as soon as the lesson is over, I will allow him to look at my notes to get the material that he is missing. I could also ask him to write down the questions that he has about missing material in his notes and I will help him individually after the lesson. I could also try to give Juan attention in other ways, such as calling on him in class when he raises his hand or encouraging him when I catch him being good. This student has so many assets to add to the class because of his intelligence and his good nature. He always seems to misbehave in his own way when some of the other students are vying for their attention through their own avenues.

Another area would be what I might start to say to the student. I could send an "I" message to Juan. An example of an "I" message in this instance would be, "Juan, when you interrupt me more than once during class, I feel discouraged because I can't get through the material that I need to cover. Is there some way that we can solve this problem to eliminate so many disruptions?" This would allow Juan and I to discuss the problem and solutions to the problem privately. This is encouraging to Juan because he knows that I am trying to help him.

The next solution that comes to mind is to catch Juan being good. This is very encouraging for Juan because he knows that I am noticing the good things that he is doing in my class. When we have a good day with no interruptions, I could walk over to talk with Juan after class and comment on that fact. I could also look over his notes for him at the end of class to make sure that he has what he needs.

A final solution to my problem with Juan can be solved by allowing Juan to run errands for me, such as taking televisions back to the media center or taking the attendance to the office when the computers are down. I don't just let any of the students out of the room during class. Juan would know that he is noticed in my classroom for the good things that he does.

My strengths as a teacher in dealing with this situation with Juan are that I am caring, persistent, and willing to change my ways. I care about my students and the learning atmosphere in my classroom. I know that there is a problem and I know that I need to find something that works to solve it. I am also persistent. If one technique does not work, I will continue to try until something solves the problem. This flexibility shows that I realize that sometimes it is not only the students that need to change to solve a classroom problem.

Comment: The teacher begins with a clear understanding of the general dynamic in the classroom — high school students in groups, but all seeking to gain attention. The focus on one student with a relatively mild misbehavior generates many possible alternatives for the teacher. This teacher sees strengths within herself and finds ways to use them with students.

Case 7: Jen

Age and setting: Jen is a 15-year-old in tenth grade.

Behavior: She is in my third block geometry course. I have been having trouble with Jen disrupting class by asking irrelevant questions while I am teaching. Since Jen is disrupting me from effectively teaching the other 27 students in the class, this is a teacher-owned problem. When the problem is "fixed," she will refrain from disrupting the class by asking only relevant questions. In the past, I have only been able to fix the problem for a limited amount of time. She might not disrupt for a half-hour or even the rest of the class period, but she has always resumed her disruptive behavior after a period of time.

When Jen disrupts class by asking irrelevant questions. I feel very annoyed. I respond by reminding her to stay focused and only ask questions about the topic at hand. Since my feeling toward her behavior was annoyance, I can pinpoint the goal of her misbehavior as a need for attention. Like the inexperienced teacher I am, I gave Jen the normal, expected response. I reminded and coaxed her. She, in turn, gave me the normal, expected response of refraining from the misbehavior temporarily and then later resuming.

Analysis: The goal of her behaviors is attention.

Alternatives

- Minimize the attention
- Distract her
- Notice appropriate behavior

Jen is a very likable student. However, as she continues this disruptive behavior, the other students in the class grow to dislike her. So, as her teacher and encourager, I have decided to try to bring out one of her strong points: she is willing to help. If she feels that she is getting attention in a positive way, she will reduce misbehavior to get attention.

My consultation group came up with three suggestions that may be effective in dealing with Jen's misbehavior. The first recommendation is to have a conference with Jen. In the conference I would let Jen know that if she has any questions that aren't about geometry to feel free to come see me before or after class, but that class time is just that, a time to learn about the topic at hand. Another suggestion was to use an "I" message to let Jen know that I feel very discouraged when she interrupts the lesson with her pointless questions. Since she is a caring individual, the "I" message may appeal to her. The third, and I believe the most effective strategy, is to enlist her help. She wants to be the center of attention, so I could use that in a positive way. I could get her to help pass out rulers, take up homework papers, or run errands. This way, she is getting positive attention from me and the other students aren't rolling their eyes at her for asking irrelevant questions. If I am able to make Jen feel "noticed" by acknowledging her positive behaviors, I think this misbehavior will be reduced if not eliminated.

Comment: The teacher benefits from a consultation group that generates alternatives. The teacher clearly understands the student's need for attention and begins to find positive alternative behaviors. Although she is an "inexperienced" teacher, she sees alternatives quickly and feels encouraged. The use of positive behaviors within the student's peer groups is an extremely effective technique at this grade level.

Case 8: Jamal

Age and setting: Jamal is a 14-year-old in the ninth grade.

Behavior: The student I chose to share with the group is Jamal. One day, earlier in the school year, Jamal was having difficulty with an algebra assignment. He wadded up his paper and threw it on the floor. Jamal also got frustrated and yelled, "I'm not doing this crap! Screw it!" My first reaction was to ask Jamal to pick up the paper. I then asked if he needed help. Jamal told me that I only confused him and he did not need help. He refused to do the work and got out a piece of paper and started drawing. I then told him I could not make him do the work, but the papers would be graded. If Jamal chose not to do his work, he would receive a zero. He decided it would be fine for him to take a zero. Jamal knows the consequences for not turning in work. Yet he chooses to not turn in his work.

Analysis: I believe he turned a display of inadequacy into a power-seeking and revenge situation. He expressed his lack of confidence by saying he could not do the work. He wanted to get out of doing the task because he was frustrated, so he decided to blow off some steam by yelling and throwing his paper. By further refusing to do his work, Jamal was trying a power-struggle situation, focusing his anger and frustration on me, the teacher. I felt a little frustrated that he got so anxious over a math problem. Jamal is typically a pleasant student that is very artistic and creative. He loves to draw sketches of objects and to create buildings.

Alternatives   There are several options that I could explore with this type of situation. One thing I would like to do is to get Jamal to complete his assignment and know that I am more than willing to help him understand a difficult problem.

- *I could ask Jamal to take a time out to cool down.* By removing Jamal from the classroom, I would also be removing the audience and allowing him to save face. Allowing Jamal to come back to class when he is ready to work on his assignment is giving him an opportunity to try again and make the right decision. Giving Jamal the choice gives him some control to correct a bad situation.
- *I could table the matter to a time later that day.* I could meet with Jamal when he is calm and discuss the effects his decisions make on his class grade. Using an "I" message to express my concern for his grade will help by not placing judgment, but rather letting him know that there are logical consequences for his behavior. I could also give him a chance to finish the paper for homework, by

getting help from a peer that lives in his unit. This is giving Jamal another opportunity to correct a bad situation.

Jamal is feeling discouraged about his problems with algebra and chose to display some misbehavior to express his feelings. I will encourage Jamal's efforts to perform the task regardless of the errors. I could make mistakes okay for Jamal and allow him to correct his errors for credit toward his papers. I will tell Jamal I understand algebra is a difficult subject and also that I expect it to be difficult for many students. This may also help relieve some of the pressure of making mistakes. One other idea that may help Jamal when he is feeling frustrated with a problem is to give him a secret signal he can use to get my attention without calling the attention of the rest of the class.

Comment: The student does not "know" how to do algebra but has taken active steps to protect his self-esteem. The revenge and power responses to the work task are accurately understood by the teacher. Alternatives that focus on the moments of misbehavior are half the solution. Some of these ideas (such as telling the student that the class is difficult) may not work immediately, but it is important to respect reasonable ideas from the teacher and allow them to explore the alternatives. The teacher also sees ways to approach Jamal when tensions are reduced.

DVD CONSULTATION CASES

Case 1

Dr. Carlson meets with a kindergarten teacher, Pat, concerned about Adolfo, a student who does not cooperate. Issues such as language barriers and insufficient testing are discussed before moving to a more helpful discussion of alternatives.

Case 2

Mother and Andy meet with Dr. Carlson about routine challenges such as chores. The preadolescent shows some recognition reflex responses to the consultant's tentative hypotheses concerning his behaviors.

Case 3

Matt, an elementary school student, discusses his daily schedule with Dr. Carlson and his father. Matt and Dad are big talkers; the session shows how to structure the consultation.

Case 4

Dr. Dinkmeyer meets with Ann Marie, a sixth-grade math teacher. The student, Gina, does not bring her book to class. This session illustrates how consultees respond to the education component of a consultation.

Case 5

Parent Consultation Group with Dr. Dinkmeyer illustrates the collaborative nature of the members. Parents contribute real examples of child behaviors while universalizing common challenges.

SUMMARY

The chapter presents case examples to illustrate a consultation method consistent with the principles outlined in the previous seven chapters. The reader is encouraged to consider how one might use these ideas in his or her own setting. When working with teachers, regardless of the setting or teacher challenge, the application of a dynamic, useful psychology in a systematic format provides effective consultation interventions.

APPENDIX I:
DVD CASE TRANSCRIPT

This is a transcript of the fourth DVD consultation — Ann Marie, a sixth-grade math teacher and her student, Gina. The session illustrates the educational nature of consultations as well as the structure of an effective consultation. Consultant and Teacher statements are numbered. A commentary track by the consultant is also available on the DVD.

C1. Hi Ann Marie, I'm Don.

T1. Hi, nice to meet you.

C2. Nice to meet you and thanks for helping us out. We're going to talk for about fifteen minutes. You're a classroom teacher or a helper to teachers, and we'd like you to pick out a student that is a challenge, and we're going to see if we can find some things that can help you with that student.

T2. Ok, that would be great.

C3. Do you have one or two that come to mind?

T3. Yes, as a matter of fact I do. Right now I am an LD resource teacher, so I go into a classroom and work with kids there and do team teaching or I take them out and work with them in small groups. I have one particularly that comes to mind, who has been diagnosed special education, and is failing just about every subject. However, its hard for me and her regular teachers to help her because she comes constantly unprepared for class, late for class, notebook, no book, no homework, loses everything. Its frustrating because she was moved into a math class that I team teach in, so that I could help her, and I can't help her if she doesn't do any work.

C4. This would be a good example to work with. And her name is …

T4. Gina.

C5. Her name is Gina, and she's in what grade again, please?

T6. Sixth grade.

C7. Ok, we have sixth grade Gina, math. All right, and you're team teaching.

T7. Uhuh.

C8. Can you think of the last time that this pattern occurred, this challenge occurred. If we ran a video camera, what would that camera see, or what would it hear?

T8. If we ran a video, it would see a student very disinterested. She — it's kind of like her — like she's at school to see her friends and socialize, you know, and learning and class work is kinda like a distraction.

C9. So at sixth grade she is about eleven, or twelve?

T9. Eleven.

C10. Has never been held back?

T10. No. And I am wondering if that's the problem, because sometimes in special education when these kids are in the system so much, they start depending on other people to bail them out … and you can help them to a certain degree … but they are learning disabled, but they aren't helpless …

C11. Okay … I think that's well said, but also what I'm hearing you say is that sometimes these students have these get out of jail, or get out of work cards … they say, "Hey, why would you expect anything from me, I'm certifiably incapable" … I think your non-verbal, head nodding as well is indicating … is this part of what is going on in Gina's head? She's saying, "Hey, why expect anything from me, I'm not one of the capable ones."

T11. It's possible. When she first came in, she was really trying.

C12. Wait, wait, she WAS trying?

T12. She was in another math class and then when we found out we had an IEP on her and she was identified with math disabilities they moved her into my math class, so that I could work with her. So she was changed in the middle of October. I met her then and told her what was happening and why she was coming into another math class, she was fine with it. She seemed to try in this new surrounding and wanting to please, then after about a month she just kind of just stopped.

C13. She just stopped? Okay.

Let's go back to today or yesterday, to a specific incident. We call those anecdotes.

I hear that she never does her work, or rarely does it. But I'd like to have one incident that would tell me what you did, what she said, literally roll the script about what happened.

T13. Okay. For instance, her math book. She can never seem to have her math book for class.

C14. The last time this happened was …?

T14. Somebody stole her math book.

C15. The last this happened …?

T15. Monday.

C16. Monday? Someone stole her math book? And what did she say to you?

T16. She said, as they all came into class and they were all working out of their math book on division and multiplication of decimals.

I said, Gina, where is your math book?

I dunno.

Is it in your locker? No. Is it in your desk? NO. Did you leave it at home?

No, Somebody stole it. My response was well …

"Why would they take your math book?"

C17. Um hu.

T17. This has happened several times since October, where she has come unprepared; she forgets it, she leaves it at home, she'll leave it in the class period three periods earlier, so now she is running out of excuses, so now it's somebody has stole it. So, ah, my solution was to borrow an extra one, instead of having her sit there ... give one on loan to her.... And I told her, you know, that she needs to look real hard for it or otherwise she may have to pay for a new one.

C18. So, what did she think about the reimbursement plan?

T18. She rolled her eyes at me, but ah, then the next day, she came in with the math book. It magically reappeared again.

C 19. It is a miracle ... the book reappeared again!

Let me go back to the time when she came in and the book wasn't there. If I can capture that moment.... If you can go back and tell me how you felt at time ... when she came in and didn't have the math book and told you that. If I can give you four choices at that time: annoyed at her, angry at her, the other is you felt very hurt, and the last is you felt like giving up on Gina. Of those four, would one of these be closer to how you felt at that time when the math book didn't appear?

T20. I would say is that I was annoyed.

C21. If that's the case, then what I'd like to do, this is a technique I'd like to use that can be pretty helpful. Let me give you a card and a pen. I have some ideas that are going on.

I think that one of the things that's going on, at least at that time, and I know there are other circumstances and all, one of the things is that I think that her goal of behavior at that time, was for attention. I'd like for you to write that down. She is looking for you to pay attention to her at that time. This is just a tentative hypothesis ... a hunch or a guess.

Another thing that would be interesting for you to think about is that no one throws away a behavior that works. And Gina has got ...

T21. That is so true what you just said. It is exactly ...

C22. Yeah, it is the case that no one throws away a behavior that works. If I went to the bank and asked for a $100 bill and they gave it to me, no questions asked, I know where I'd go if I needed money. Kids, students always do want interaction … they crave belonging and hanging out with great teachers like Anne Marie. In a bigger group, sometimes you gotta be very creative and inventive … you got to lose a book, the cat ate it. Or whatever it is. … So use behaviors that will work. And those four ideas that I used, I was trying to identify which goal of misbehavior she was pursuing. See the idea is she was going for attention. That's important information … we want to write that down … no one throws away a behavior that works. And the idea that we want to use here, Anne Marie, is that there are some things you want to STOP at the moment of misbehavior and there are some things you want to START. The STOP part would be pretty much along the lines of where you didn't accept the excuse and you got her another book, and I think that's wonderful. That was what worked? Right?

T22. Right.

C23. So that was a good thing to do. But there is a hidden message in Gina's behavior. You might imagine that she's wearing a T-shirt, "Catch me being good" "Notice me." … She's using something to get noticed and what you want to see or think about is … are there times that you might be able to catch her being good? That might be something to write down. You might say, I'm doing this 85 times a day, I've got it on video and she's looking for the 86th!

T23. Right. I've tried positive reinforcement all the time. When it was her birthday, I brought her into my room and gave her a Reese's bar or whatever. Made sure I said … Happy birthday to her. When she handed in her homework on time, good job, Gina. Asked her when she came back from break, "How was your break" … I tell her everday, have a nice evening. I do try as much positive reinformcement with these kids because with their academic abilities, they don't get a lot of it.

C24. That's exactly right. Not only do you try, I think you do. Another thing we could also do … are you interested in … how do you feel about learning? Being a teacher, are you in favor of it?

T24. Absolutely!

C25. One of the things we're learning here are there are goals of behavior … one is attention getting at least for Gina at that time.

There's another thing I'd like to add in terms of positive reinforcement … you use that to motivate?

T25. Yeah.

C26. There's an additional area I'd like to open up for your consideration, which is called encouragement. There are all sorts of things I can give to you that relate to the idea of encouragement. Because at times I think Gina, rightly so, sees herself as a discouraged child…. If you were where she is, labeled as she is, that's very discouraging. They're not nominating you for a Nobel prize … they are tracking you in another life direction. So one of the things you might want to write down in addition to positive reinforcement. Don't give up any of that. I also want you to look at some ways to begin to encourage Gina and the other students in your opportunities in your teaching. It's called encouragement. The idea is that when a student doesn't move, they're discouraged. It takes courage to move from here to a place where they want to do the work. Write down some ways to encourage Gina. It's another motivational technique and frankly, it's one that a lot of teachers haven't been exposed to a lot, it's not like they've thought about it and said … no, don't want any part of that. Just hasn't really been talked about very much. It's a very powerful force, especially with children who are very discouraged. Dr. Dreikurs had an interesting phrase, "even the incorrigible are encourageable" and he said "a child needs encouragement like a plant needs water." Part of what goes on in our classrooms today is that there's not enough watering, or encouragement of the students and we could talk about a lot of things. What's one of Gina's strengths?

T26. One of her strengths?

C27. Yeah, what's an asset?

T27. I would say is that she is very good at writing and drawing. She's definitely a very good artist.

C28. One of the things you'd want to write down and it would be your creative opportunity is to find ways to let her use her assets or strengths. That could be very encouraging. I know it won't happen in all circumstances, but it is a way to recognize and let her use her strengths or assets. Her assets can be very encouraging.

In the time we have to summarize, we have a wonderful example of a sixth grader who has a purpose in her behavior with the book is not showing up, and really what at least to this point in time, we're going to see it as a "hey, notice me" kind of signal and you're already not buying it ... you're saying, hey, I'm going to get you other ways to do the book work. But you're also going to try to find ways to "catch Gina being good." And, as it relates to the idea of encouragement, one of the ways to get great momentum and movement out of children, is to make the agenda things they are interested in. With math, it may be hard to knit together, but with some time, I think we could work on that.

Just to finish up, I always like to ask the people (teachers) I'm working with, whether they could take one or two sentences and finish them for us: I learned ... and I will.... Something you learned in the conversation about yourself.

T28. I learned that Gina's behavior has to do with attention. And I will from now on realize that it's important to encourage her and incorporate her assets into the lesson or homework to make her feel more in control or ...

C29. more empowered ... or more belonging? I couldn't say it any better. ... You've helped me out.... Thank you.

T29. Thank you.

APPENDIX II:
THE "C" GROUP

"C" groups are concerned with three professional roles within the school—the counselor, the administrator, and teachers. Few teacher education programs or traditional school in-services are similar to the "C" group. Components of the "C" group are:

- collaboration
- consultation
- clarification
- confrontation
- concern
- confidentiality
- commitment
- communication
- change
- cohesion

The group is both didactic (teaching new skills) and experiential (sharing feelings). The content comes from sharing concerns and the process involves analysis of the purpose of behavior, identification of assets, and contracts for change.

Consultants need to thoroughly understand the purpose and the value of working with teachers in "C" groups. For example, many counselors are receiving numerous teacher-referred students as discipline problems. Teacher groups can reduce the pressure to "fix and return" these students because sharing problem-solving skills with teachers will lead to reduction in the number of student referrals.

Most classroom behavior problems are interpersonal in nature. Students represent one half of the teacher–student relationship. This emphasizes the need to work with teachers — the adult half of the relationship. By stimulating positive interaction among teachers and between the counselor and teachers, each "C" group indirectly reaches hundreds of children. Although counseling and psychological services to students and other elements within the school have their own value, teacher groups often are the only direct and tangible evidence of these services to teachers. The consultant can use this rationale to enthusiastically communicate to administrators and the teaching staff the value of consultant directed teacher groups.

Administrative support of the group is essential. Principals should be aware of the purpose and merit of the group and encourage participation from staff. The educational and voluntary nature of the "C" group should be emphasized. From the administration standpoint, "C" groups can provide an effective training experience in reducing classroom behavior problems. They increase teachers' disciplinary effectiveness. The "C" group also stresses related elements of effective teaching, such as how to motivate and encourage students.

Teachers themselves need to be fully apprised of the nature of the group. "C" groups and similar teacher services can be misunderstood and perceived as therapy or an indication of ineffective teaching. They actually represent an extremely valuable laboratory for education, sharing of experiences, and resolving of common classroom challenges.

Organizing the "C" Group

Each "C" group consists of four to six teachers who meet one hour each week for a minimum of 6 to 8 weeks. Groups often meet before school, at mutual lunch hours, or during the planning periods, both during and after school. Administrative support is necessary to approve the time and space needed, along with appropriate changes in schedules and responsibilities. The "C" group is not a sensitivity group nor is it an administration-backed prescription to cure the school's "worst" teachers. The first group contains a cross-section of the staff including those who have social and professional power within the school.

A demonstration and brief explanation at a staff meeting can be the first stimulation of interest. Deliberate development of teacher interest and knowledge of the "C" group is essential. At this meeting or whenever groups are formed, each member must make a commitment to attend all group meetings. Additionally, teachers should not join a "C" group after the first meeting. Instead, their interest can be the basis of forming the next "C" group.

A "C" group should be a heterogeneous blend of experience, orientations, and skills. The common denominator is the age of the students each teacher represents, because behavior problems are often similar at certain age and grade levels. A group of fourth-grade teachers, for example, more easily identifies with the classrooms involved than does a group of first- and fifth-grade teachers. Nevertheless, primary, intermediate, and junior high teachers can be of assistance to each other.

"C" groups begin with the consultant's presentation of an Adlerian theory of behavior and misbehavior. Each group member must understand these principles of misbehavior and goal identification. The four goals of misbehavior (attention, power, revenge, and display of inadequacy) and subsequent teacher actions in response to these misbehaviors are the foundation of the group's knowledge. This allows each teacher in the group to have a common base from which to understand student behavior and misbehavior.

The consultant structures the group by suggesting the group adhere to the following guidelines:

- Stay on the topic.
- Become involved in the discussion.
- Share the time.
- Be patient — take one step at a time.
- Encourage each other.
- Be responsible for your own behavior.
- What we say here stays here.
- The leader is a mandated reporter.

Once the group has this common knowledge of behavior, solving misbehavior problems is a primary focus of the group. Each week time is allotted to teachers for presentation of a student behavior problem.

The "C" group offers the following:

- A theory of human behavior that speaks directly to classroom misbehavior.
- A technique for identifying student misbehavior goals.
- A realization by teachers that goal identification is based on their reactions and feelings about misbehavior; for example, a specific reaction such as annoyance indicates a specific misbehavior goal (attention). In this systematic and lawful understanding of human behavior, "answers" are available to every teacher who comes to recognize the purpose of misbehavior.

- Suggestions for teachers' reactions to misbehavior that do not inadvertently "feed" the misbehavior's purpose. Many initial or conventional responses to student misbehavior suffer from this unintentional dynamic. For example, a show of force or punishment in response to power-oriented misbehavior only impresses and reinforces the student's belief in the importance of power. Paying attention to attention-getting misbehavior meets the goal (attention) of that misbehavior.
- A procedure whereby teachers can share misbehavior incidents within a group to identify the goal and corrective actions.
- A realization that teacher-student conflict presents an opportunity for teachers to change when teachers often have assumed previously that their verbal commands produce such change in students.

The consultant's leadership in the "C" group begins with an effective presentation of the curriculum and then structures the group into a problem-solving and follow-through procedures. Each group member is the focus for approximately 10 to 15 minutes. A specific incident and anecdotes are presented and worked on by the group. The leader is not an expert to which these problems are referred. Group members work with each other and the leader encourages this interaction throughout the group sessions. The teachers thus develop problem-solving skills and the ability to consult with one another specifically and effectively. This approach has been labeled the "C" group because factors which make it effective begin with the letter "C."

1. *Collaboration.* The group collaborates and works together on mutual concerns. The leader has an equal position. There are not superior/inferior relationships between the leader and the group or between members of the group. They are in the group for the purpose of mutual help.
2. *Consultation* is both received and provided by the teachers. The interaction that occurs within the group between the leader and the members helps group members to become aware of new approaches with students.
3. *Clarification.* The group members clarify for other members their belief systems, their feelings, and the congruency or incongruency between their behavior, beliefs, and feelings.
4. *Confrontation* makes the group more productive insofar as it produces more realistic and honest feedback. The expectation is that each individual will see him- or herself, his or her purposes, attitudes, and beliefs, and will be willing to confront

other members about their psychological makeup. Members in the group confront each other because they want to help each other to become more effective.

5. *Concern.* The group is concerned and shows that it cares. This concern leads members to collaborate, consult, clarify, and confront in order to develop the human potential of both students and group members.

6. *Confidentiality.* The group is confidential in the sense that whatever is discussed within the group stays within the group. The purpose is to be mutually helpful, not to generate gossip.

7. *Commitment.* The group helps individuals to develop a commitment to change. Participants in the group become involved in helping other members to recognize that they really can change only themselves. They may come to the group expecting to change students, but they soon learn that they must develop a specific commitment to take action before the next C group that will attempt to change their approach to the problem.

8. *Communication.* The group is a new channel for communication insofar as it communicates not only ideas but feelings, attitudes, and beliefs. Members become involved with each other as persons.

9. *Change.* The group members recognize that changing students' behavior often requires that they change their beliefs, attitudes, and procedures.

10. *Cohesion.* The group is most effective when there is cohesion and the members work together as a team.

TOPIC INDEX

AUTHOR INDEX